Testimonials

You get to be the active participant in how you choose your healthcare providers — I can only share with you, I met Dr. Jay Shetlin after a terrible cycling accident, and after learning his practices and following his guidelines first hand, I saw direct benefits and plan on utilizing these practices throughout the rest of my life. The practical advice and implementation of the treatments in this book, will change your outlook on how you choose your own future health initiatives. Great read! ~*Teri Klug, President Strategic Development*

I recently attended one of Dr. Shetlin's dinner classes where he spoke about sleep and maximizing REM sleep. With no exaggeration, the quick bit of knowledge I attained was life changing. Since the class I can honestly say I've implemented many things into my daily routine. His chiropractic work changed my life, but just as much so did this class. I truly believe Dr. Shetlin's primary focus is to share his knowledge of Holistic Health and Wellness with the world. ~ *Nicholas Santillanes-Young*

My husband and I attended one of Dr. Shetlin's heath classes. I have to say, it was very informative regarding health, nutrition, exercise and chiropractic care. Being a skeptical person and working in hospitals for the past 10 years, I never believed chiropractic care could be so beneficial to the human body. I am now seeing a chiropractor on a regular basis and I feel absolutely amazing. ~ *Janette W.*

My family and I have attended Dr. Shetlin's dinner classes several times. In fact I have brought many of my friends and co-workers to the classes. They loved it! I love it enough to keep going back each year and I pick up something new every time I go. Listen, learn, implement, benefit. The things we have learned has helped our entire family live healthier and happier. ~ *Becky Robison*

FUTURE HEALTH

SOLVING THE HEALTH AND WEALTH CONUNDRUM

FUTURE HEALTH

SOLVING THE HEALTH AND WEALTH CONUNDRUM

Turn-key techniques for daily living that empower individuals and families to affordably navigate the health pitfalls of our day without jeopardizing their financial future.

South Jordan, UT

www.drjayshetlin.com

Dedication

For my wife Shannon,

and my awesome kids

Savanna,

Joshua,

Colby,

and Harrison

"Life is for Living, Laughing and Loving!"

-Ed Forman

Thanks to:
Patrice Hunt, Shantelle Pratt, Tracy Taylor, Dr. David Clement, Dr. Peter Carr, John and Raylene Barnes for input and support. Special Thanks to my mentors: Mark Victor Hansen, Ed Forman, and Doctors Fabrizio Mancini, CJ Mertz, Andrew Hatch, Rick Wren, Gilles Lamarche, Gen Orlowsky, Dan Murphy, John Demartini, Charles Ward, Bruce Parker, and Jim Sigafoose, DD Palmer and BJ Palmer for the inspiration.

PREFACE

Health is a journey. However, we often desire instant gratification and expect results as soon as we put any effort. A muscle isn't strengthened by inactivity, our health is the same, it has to be challenged, allowed to respond, adapt and then become stronger through the process.

When we decide to make our health a priority, we think differently, we act differently and our potential increases. Our relationships are deeper and longer lasting, our energy improves, the connections we make are greater and our life experiences are richer.

Use this book as a guide, a resource, for motivation and for implementation. Successful people do what unsuccessful people do not want to do. So be successful, be consistent, be focused and achieve what you deserve. You are amazing, you are capable of great health and a great life; decide now to improve your health, your life and your legacy. And, enjoy the journey!

Kristina A. Stitcher, D.C.

Pediatric and Family Wellness Chiropractor

International Speaker and Lecturer

Mentor and Coach

CONTENTS

This book is meant to be
read, highlighted and re-read
so an individual can
little by little
apply techniques
to form habits
that will help
maximize their life's
fulfilment and happiness.

INTRODUCTION

In 2000 I had a positive life-changing experience in which I had attended a seminar with speakers including: Mark Victor Hansen, Senator Ed Forman, Dr. James Sigafoose, and several other prominent individuals that dedicate their time and talents to improving the lives of everyone they touch. Granted they do it to make a living but it is a "give to get" mentality rather than a "what's in it for me" way of thinking.

This book is one aspect of my attempt to reach more individuals in a like fashion offering life-improving techniques to help anyone in any situation make each day better for themselves and those around them. Herein are tools or techniques to help individuals stay the course of health and prosperity or rise from the ashes of destitution and despair.

This book is an easy read. It is not written to be wordy, fancy or full of fluff. It is simple and to the point with several personal experiences in the mix. It is not a textbook but more of a conversation with you, the reader that should be revisited often.

Dr. R. Jay Shetlin

TECHNIQUES FOR ADVANCED LIVING

When we study the most successful and influential people in the world, both past and present, the majority have a number of traits or habits in common. I call these "Techniques for Advanced Living." This book will address a number of health and wealth tips that, when applied, can develop personal programming that is incredibly and positively life-changing.

There are few physical differences between the average person and a great spiritual, political, financial, or motivational leader. The differences between average and great individuals can be found in the way they think, the habits they have developed, and the principles they live. "Great people" aren't shaped by a single event. Rather, they come about as a result of the little things they do, day in and day out.

To you and I, our health and wealth (not just financial wealth) are two of the fundamental elements directly influencing our ability to personally thrive, and positively influence the lives of others.

In order to solve the "Health and Wealth Conundrum" of our day and maximize our "Future Health," we must focus on "the individual." A person may not be able to incorporate ALL the suggestions in this book in a single read or even in a month of effort. However, I guarantee the more you apply the "Techniques for Advanced Living," within this book, the more empowered you will become, mentally, physically, spiritually, and financially.

HARRISON• PART I

April 7th 2002, 9:36am: It had been a rough night. Just three days after the delivery of our 4th child, I held little Harrison in my arms knowing something was seriously wrong. He seemed fine initially, but now he wouldn't eat; he was prone to arching his back rather than curling up in a fetal position like most babies, and he winced every time we changed his position. It was as if the slightest movement was causing him pain. Other signs were setting off my doctor-warning-signals that this perfect little baby's life was in danger. I was suspecting spinal meningitis, a deadly bacterial infection around the brain and spinal cord, which can be fatal within 48 hours.

I called our pediatrician at an early Sunday hour and explained the symptoms over the phone. He too was concerned, enough so that he said he would meet us at the hospital right away.

The hospital staff buzzed around as concern grew for our newborn with possible spinal meningitis. They all understood the seriousness of this illness, with its morbid outcome, and the small window of time in which to diagnose and treat before it was too late. My wife was pretty distraught at the sight surrounding her tiny infant…she had to step outside the room. We performed a spinal tap, an uncomfortable procedure which draws fluid from the spinal cord to test for bacterial count. It would tell us if the meningitis was viral, meaning not so dangerous; or bacterial — potentially deadly.

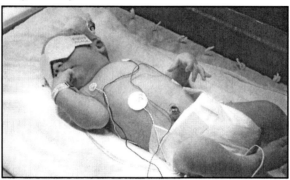

Once we drew the tiny vile of fluid from Harrison's back, it was obvious, even to the naked eye, that something was amiss. Spinal fluid should be a clear liquid, but Harrison's was a milky color from all the white blood cells trying to fight a bacterial infection. I didn't need a lab to tell me there was a problem. A big problem. Neither did our pediatrician. With a sigh of distress, I mentally calculated how it had been nearly 36 hours since we first noticed any signs of trouble. At first, the signs could have meant a number of things. Now it was clear a serious fight for survival was taking place within this little body. The clock was ticking and every minute was stacking against Harrison's chance at life…

ANATOMY-PHYSIOLOGY 101

The human body is of perfect design. It is a micro-universe made up of trillions of living (and some dead) cells. Miraculously, the human body can survive with minimal effort; but to thrive requires some understanding of how the body works so we can better preserve it. If you are a religious individual, you might look at your body as a gift from a loving God in Heaven. In the Bible He tells us "Our body is a temple," and should we choose not to respect and take care of our body, there are consequences.[1] We have a responsibility to know how our body optimally works and, how to take care of it.

Your body has an innate intelligence that flows throughout. It controls and coordinates everything that happens in the body. Information between the brain and every cell within the body works to maintain optimal function, regulate temperature, heart-rate, digest food, fight off infection and much more. Every cell, organ and tissue is controlled by the master system which is the nervous system. It is fundamentally important to minimize interference to the nervous system, as will be explained throughout this book. Equally important, the body needs proper nutrients provided and toxins avoided. Naturally, the body needs proper rest for rejuvenation and plenty of movement (exercise) on a daily basis. Together these are some of the basic necessities to help the body heal itself and thrive.

Health does not come in a bottle, pill or potion.

A few examples that directly affect the health of our body in a POSITIVE way are things such as a properly functioning nervous system, nutritional foods, exercise, stretching, proper rest, loving relationships, managing stress, and financial peace of mind.

Many things have a direct NEGATIVE affect upon our health and body including trauma, toxins and **stress.** Let's face it, for many of us, stress is unavoidable. However, it can be properly managed, thus minimizing its overall effect on us. Unfortunately, stress can also be poorly managed, thereby exaggerating its negative affect on our life. *Lack of exercise* has a negative affect on our health. Consuming *toxins* such as chemicals in our food, alcohol, chewing tobacco, tobacco smoke, pollutants in the air, and drugs of any kind (yes, even prescription and over-the-counter-drugs) have a profoundly negative effect on the body. A poor diet, low in healthy foods can also be toxic. *Traumas* to the body such as slips, falls, car accidents, work injuries, poor posture, repetitive micro-traumas, even the birth process, can be excessively traumatic. Birth, of course, can be traumatic to both mom and baby. Even a "normal birth" can be extremely dangerous to the baby if there is any pulling or rotation applied to the head and neck in the birthing process.

These traumas have individual importance, but it is critical to point out that the majority of them directly affect the nervous system, which controls all other systems, organs, and cells of the body.

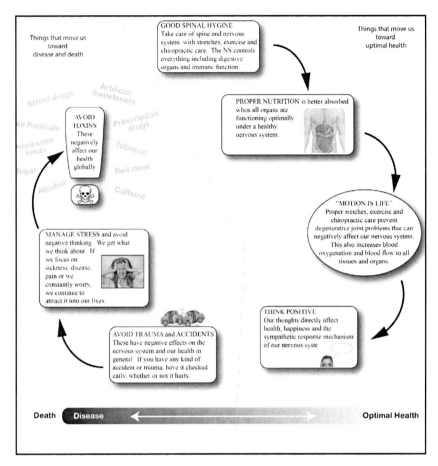

Simply put, **Thoughts, Traumas,** and **Toxins** are the primary components that most influence our nervous system thereby affecting our health.[2]

The three "T's," Thoughts, Traumas, and Toxins are the key groups leading AWAY from health and TOWARD disease. They are the three most common categories that affect our nervous system, thereby directly affecting our health. With thoughts, however, the door swings both ways. Our thoughts can be one of our basic stumbling blocks preventing us from having better health, losing

7

weight, even finding happiness each day. OR our positive focused thoughts can be our saving grace to deal with circumstances, challenges, pain and sickness. MOST IMPORTANTLY, POSITIVE THOUGHT PATTERNS HELP ATTRACT BETTER HEALTH AND FINANCIAL ABUNDANCE.

The human body is truly a miracle! On the day of conception two cells met — a single egg and a single sperm. Yes, millions of sperm cells were on the scene, but only one was able to penetrate the egg, thus fertilizing it. These two cells merged to form a single cell, then began to divide — two, four, eight, sixteen — in the end creating trillions of cells in the body at the time of birth.

Part of this miracle is the fact that each cell divided perfectly! No sloppy carbon copies, but perfect duplicates, one after the other. Then another miracle took place when the innate intelligence began to orchestrate groups of cells to become the heart, bones, kidneys, etc. The first noticeable formation of any cells into a structure was on day 11.

Day 11 is remarkable because it is when we first see the 'primitive streak' begin to take shape. Before any other organ or system is made, the brain and spinal cord, (i.e. the nervous system) is formed. It is the first *system* to develop. It then influences all the other developing organs and systems. The nervous system controls and coordinates every other organ, system or function that will ever take place in your body. Every <u>living</u> cell in the body has nerve innervations.

With all the cells, organs, and systems in place our body is ready to grow, adapt, and thrive in an ever-changing environment. The complexity of these electro-chemical events that occur on a daily basis in our personal micro-universe, called a body, is nothing short of miraculous. Trillions of nerve impulses take place in a single human body each day. These impulses electro-chemical communications between the brain and target tissues travel at over 290 miles per hour. They orchestrate an amazing balance of chemistry, hormones, temperature regulation, pH balance, stomach acidity, gas exchange (oxygen / carbon dioxide), and locomotion, just to name a few functions. Of course, most of this work takes place without us ever consciously thinking about it. That is the wonder of our nervous system. Our senses (sight, smell, taste, touch, and hearing) allow us to interpret and interact with our surroundings, as well as each other, all under the control of the nervous system. Organs function to break down food and absorb nutrients, expel waste, filter the blood, and fight bacteria, viruses and disease, all under the watchful function of the nervous system.

Simply put, if we take care of our nervous system, it will take care of us. When we do not maintain a healthy nervous system, any number of problems, symptoms, or diseases present themselves.

It is surprising to me that research by a medical doctor performed back in 1921 is not common knowledge throughout the world. The Windsor Study should be addressed in every basic anatomy class.

The Windsor Study

Henry Windsor, MD[3] Just prior to receiving his degree, Dr. Windsor was preparing to graduate from medical school and needed to prepare his final thesis paper. There was a buzz in the medical community about the hypothesis that degenerated or pinched nerves between the spine and target organs may lead to disease. Dr. Windsor proposed he be allowed to dissect several bodies of individuals who had died from various diseases to see if there was any validity to this discussion. Permission was granted and he performed his dissections on over 100 bodies. The subjects had died due to diseases such as lymphoma, kidney failure, liver disease, lung cancer etc. To his surprise he found that the nerve between the diseased organ and the spine was degenerated in nearly 100% of the cases!

Other key points made in the Windsor study include:

- Curvatures of the spine adversely affect the sympathetic nervous system

- The sympathetic nervous system controls the blood supply to the viscera (organs) and is, therefore, related to all manner of visceral diseases or, "the ordinary diseases of adult life."

- Visceral diseases and pathology can be traced back to segmental levels of the spine with nearly 100% accuracy.

- Abnormal curves of the spine precede organ disease.

- Stiff distorted spines cause sympathetic irritation, vascular spasm, arterial hardening and old age follows.

- Spinal disease precedes old age or causes old age, in other words, a person is as old as his/her spine because it directly affects their nervous system.

How important is the vitality and function of the nervous system in our overall health? Clearly, if there is interference to the nervous system, diminishing the brain's ability to properly communicate and control organs and tissues, it can lead to disease or even premature death.

As stated earlier — Thoughts, Traumas and Toxins are the three T's that most directly affect the nervous system thereby affecting our development, health, and quality of life.

Footnotes:

1. 1 Corinth. (3:16-17)
2. DD Palmer, the Father of Chiropractic
3. Medical Times, November 1921, pp. 1-7

THOUGHTS

If your thoughts are not in-line with your most basic wants and desires, the simplest of attainable goals become virtually unachievable.[4] From a doctor and health coach perspective, **if your thoughts are focused on pain, sickness, problems, debt or disease rather than health, happiness, longevity, prosperity or gratitude, neither myself, nor any other doctor, will be able to help you obtain the optimal health you are capable of having!**

Simply put, thoughts lead to actions or outcomes. We must be conscious of our thoughts and keep them in check with what we truly want in life.

No doubt, each one of us is on a different mental, spiritual, and physical level. Some of us simply need to be better educated on what is good for us and receive some loving guidance in the right direction. Others are actually sick, or in pain, and the "diseases" or "challenges" we face somehow serve us. If they are serving us on some basic level we may not be willing, or able, to let them go. Let me clarify this. If an ailment provides us with *attention* that we desire on some subconscious level; or if it provides an *excuse,* whether consciously recognized or subconsciously felt; if it helps us avoid something we don't like e.g. work or some other responsibility, then the ailment is serving us.

11

If you are sick, have chronic pain, want to lose weight but can't and have "tried everything" with no success, the next paragraph is for you.

Imagine I am looking you right in the eyes… I am telling you honestly and compassionately… *with every effort you make to focus more on uplifting thoughts and less on problems, less on pain or disease, less on financial woes; your health will literally begin to change for the better. True health and wellness starts within. **You, and only you, are responsible for your health.** Not your mom, not your doctor, not the pill or potion your doctor prescribed, not your insurance provider, not your personal trainer, not you spouse, not your kids…You…You…You. In 99% of cases, there are things you can do to feel better and maximize your health. But you must have your 'headspace' right. Work on your thoughts. The right thoughts will lead the way. Positive thoughts will clear the path for the flesh to follow. Verbally tell yourself what you truly want and those words will become your reality. The Good Book says; "The word was and the word became flesh." I can look at you and honestly say; "I know you can do it!" You just need to know you can do it!*

Dr. B.J. Palmer, "The Developer" of Chiropractic put it simply; "Above, down, inside, out!" All healing happens above, down, inside, out. Mentally, it starts from our thoughts and travels down to our body. Physiologically from the central computer - the brain, down the spinal cord and out to every cell, organ, and tissue of the body.

How powerful are our thoughts in shaping our lives and our world? Infinitely!

Every action is preceded by a thought.

Everything created was first a thought, then it was made manifest in the physical.

There is incredible power in writing down our thoughts (goals), in other words, the positive things we want. This simple step begins the magic universal transformation of energy to help us begin to achieve the things we want the most. There are countless books on this topic.1 However, my goal is to make it easy for anyone to understand, implement, and share this information with friends and family to better their lives.

Imagine an architect having a great idea for a building, but all he does is show up at the construction site to make it happen. He is missing a vital step. He needs to write down his idea by drawing out the plan. Once it is written down, not only does this trigger the universal "law of attraction," but it also makes it possible for other people to physically help him. With plans that are written, others can now do their part to make the architect's building actually come into being. Synergy! It is amazing.

For personal goals you don't need to share them with others like an architect shares his plans with the construction workers. Laying out your thoughts and dreams on paper really helps universal forces line up with you to make them physically come true.

What we think about can empower us with the fuel for success. Unfortunately, the wrong thoughts can completely drain us of energy, and divert us from the things we truly want.

Like attracts Like. "Whatever the conscious mind thinks and believes, the subconscious identically creates." *~Brian Adams*

Pave the way with positive thoughts.

It is imperative we make a conscious effort to think about the things we want rather than thinking about what we don't want. We become our most dominant thoughts. Are you thinking about health, wealth and happiness?

I would like to share a couple of stories, — one fictional, one factual — to illustrate this point.

The frog story…

Once upon a time there was a pond near to a steep hill. The local frogs decided to have a race to the top.

The participants lined up and on the count of three took off as fast as they could. The strongest frogs took an early lead but as they began the climb, the difficulty they faced soon began to wear on them. They slowed and struggled. Frogs from the back, pacing themselves, began to catch up.

The hill was precipitous and the onlookers began to question the very possibility of completing such a climb. "It is impossible," shouted a frog from the crowd of onlookers. "I don't think anyone will be able to do it," shouted another.

The competing frogs continued to push onward and upward. Several became too weak or tired to continue, stopping in their tracks with fatigue. One little frog from the back gradually passed them.

"Come back to the pond, it was a silly idea," shouted another spectator. Jumping and shouting, another in the crowd said, "Quit now while you have the strength to return!"

One by one, the competing frogs stopped the climb. Even the stronger frogs were dropping out of the race. The hill was simply steeper and more challenging than they had thought. Surprisingly the one little frog would not give up...he just kept climbing. Nearing the top the little frog's legs were shaking with fatigue.

"For the love of all that is green and slimy! It is too hard! Come back," shouted a frog from the crowd.

But the little frog pushed on. Finally reaching the top of the hill, he looked back down at the pond and collapsed with exhaustion. The crowd was hopping and screaming with excitement! "He did it! We thought it was impossible! He did it!"

Later, the frog returned to the pond, and the victory party held in his favor. As he approached, the local frogs smiled and greeted him, many asking, "How did you do it? We thought it

was impossible. Didn't you hear us screaming to come back?"
The little frog just smiled looking at each frog thankfully, but said
nothing. The little frog's mom hopped over and gave him a big
victory hug then turned to the crowd and said, "He can't hear
you; he's deaf."

Now, because that little frog thought deep down that his goal was
achievable, *he was focused;* and his thoughts were not tainted by
the comments of others, he was able to see beyond what the crowd
could see, he pushed beyond where his competitors faced limits or
fatigue. He was running entirely on positive fuel.

Now for the true story.

Shannon was only 2½ years old when she contracted Spinal
Meningitis. After a fierce battle for her life, using the strongest
antibiotics available at the time, doctors ultimately told her
parents that they didn't think she would make it through the
night. Her Grandfather laid his hands on her tiny head and gave
her a blessing. All the family could do was pray and wait.

Nothing short of a miracle, little Shannon pulled through. Soon
the family noticed changes in the little girl. She regressed and was
no longer potty-trained, she could not talk and did not respond
when spoken to...she had lost her hearing...all of it!

Her parents took her to several specialists to find out what would
be the best course of education for this precious child. The doctors
advised that her learning skills were sharp and because she had
already begun forming the nerve pathways for speech and sound
recognition, she would be able to talk and read lips with the right
speech therapist. This advice was followed. Shannon would spend
her summer breaks learning to lip read the vocabulary she would
need the next year in school.

Something that for many of us may seem like a handicap, developed into "normal" for little Shannon. Then the real miracles began to happen...In the 4th grade her best friend saw an advertisement to join the drill team. She invited Shannon to go with her. Shannon's mother opposed the idea at first but with perseverance, little Shannon was able to convince her mom to let her try dance. She excelled! Later she tried out for "Stars" a drill team and excelled. In high school she made the Bountiful High School drill team. They took the state championship both years she was on the team. In college she performed with the University of Utah Drill Team. During Shannon's dance career she performed with her team at half-time for the San Francisco 49ers, the Rams, and at the Pro-bowl in Hawaii.

(Imagine, what an incredible feat it must be to keep perfect time with 24 young women all without hearing a single beat of the music. Some might say, "well she could feel the bass of the music." No. Especially when kicking and jumping in the air. It is simply not possible.)

However, along the lines of feeling the music...

In the 4th grade while visiting her cousin, Shannon sat next to her at the piano. With her foot pressed against base of the piano, she could feel the music her cousin was playing. She had the strongest urge to learn to play the piano. Not being able to hear the music, it was only natural that her mother was hesitant at the request for lessons. Once again, Shannon persisted. With her mother's support, she began piano lessons. Shannon spent 5 years learning the art of music through the piano. She would use one foot pressed against the base of the piano to feel the music and one to control the foot pedals.

The beauty of Shannon's story is this: YOU REALLY <u>CAN</u> DO ANYTHING YOU SET YOUR MIND TO, regardless of what you *perceive* as obstacles. Most of the obstacles we face begin and end within the 6 inches *between* our ears, our "headspace." In Shannon's case, it has been a distinct advantage not to be able to hear when people might say, "you won't be able to do that." Or "Come back! Don't try!! It's impossible!"

Shannon has grown to be a woman with many strengths and qualities. She is, in fact, so amazing that I decided to marry her. I honestly believe that an advantage she had over you and I is the fact that she could not hear during those critical developmental years. Growing up, most people hear the words, "You can't," "Don't do that," "It's impossible," "Don't bother," countless times. These words seep into our subconscious mind and impede our possibilities. Shannon clearly encountered these words much less frequently than the average child. Continual negativity can deflate ambition and 'stick-to-it-ness.'

My advice... **Turn a "deaf ear" to negativity and focus on the positive. That is one of the greatest strengths we can acquire in this life.**

Avoiding negativity.

There is a saying that many have heard: "attitude equals altitude." There isn't a truer statement as far as getting what you want in life. If you have a goal to quit smoking, lose weight, or run a marathon, those are great goals. If your friends and family are incessantly telling you how impossible it is for you to accomplish what you desire, the negativity can sink into your subconscious thoughts and defeat you before you begin. Worse yet, if YOU are continually putting yourself down with 'negative self-talk' this destructive habit is preventing you from excelling, and will eventually destroy the good things in your life. Train yourself to have positive self-talk.

It is vitally important to surround yourself with "can-do" people, those that support you in your aspirations.

The book, *As a Man Thinketh,* states, that it is our thoughts of worry, stress, lack and anxiety that begins or fuels the process of disease in our body. *"The body is a servant of the mind. Sickly thoughts and fear cause disease and kill. Anxiety demoralizes the whole body and lays it open for disease. Change of diet will not help a man who will not change his thoughts. When a man (or woman) has pure thoughts he no longer desires impure food. If you want to perfect your body, guard your mind."*[5]

I would like to tell you about Adriana. Statistically speaking, one out of two people in America and most of Europe, die of cancer. So chances are you know someone with cancer or who has had cancer. Someone with a positive attitude about life and living is far more likely to beat cancer than someone who harbors worry, stress, and anxiety. I have met many people who when faced with cancer said, "not me, I am going to beat this challenge…I have a family, I love life, I have a hundred reasons to live!" Those are the ones that beat cancer. Adriana, a patient that would visit our clinic regularly in Portugal, had a fantastic attitude. Facing cancer for the second time in her life, she said, "Hey, I am going to eat better and do what I can to help my body. There is no sense letting a single great day go by with me feeling sorry for myself or worrying about tomorrow. I must live, *to live,*" she said. She began receiving chemotherapy, Chiropractic care, began eating better, walking, visiting friends, traveling, and she is now enjoying every moment of every day with an incredible attitude. (2007 — Since starting to write the first edition of this book, Adriana has beaten cancer for the second time and is taking more preventative steps with diet, nutrition and Chiropractic care. HOWEVER, HER ATTITUDE THROUGH THE PROCESS WAS VITAL).

What happens with negative thoughts?

I have a friend who lost his father, Fred, some years ago. Fred was still quite young when he died. People described him as, "a man with many friends, active in his community, including community leadership, and a host to many social events." Physically, for most of his life anyway, he was strong and of great stature. He was, however, a heavy drinker and smoker. That being said, his body was constantly challenged to cleanse itself of excess toxins. It is important to point out that Fred's father died of complications from prostate cancer when he was young. It is possible this loss altered Fred's mental programming. I say this because Fred had been telling his son, my friend, since his own father died that he would die soon. "Son, I don't have many years left and I want you to know I love you." Fred would say. The son, of course, appreciated the father telling him that he loved him, but why all this talk of not having many years left? Fred was only in his forties! The father and son lived in different parts of the country and only saw each other a couple of times per year. The son recalls those words escaped his father's lips quite frequently when they were together. Years later, just as the son was graduating from college, his father died of prostate cancer at the young age of 55. The father had been 'programming' himself with this negative disease-based thinking for years and years. Unfortunately for Fred, his family, and his community, Fred got exactly what he was thinking about.

Of course, not every time someone has an ailment or disease to battle is it entirely thought-related. But clearly our thoughts do have a direct impact on our health, for good or bad.

If there are things you DON'T want in your life, then I suggest you NOT waste your time thinking about them! Sometimes it is difficult. In extreme cases, professional counseling may be in order. But the more POSITIVE things you can put into your daily consciousness the better!

Now, I'll briefly address "The Law of Attraction," then we'll come back to how thoughts affect our physiology.

Some authors anchor thoughts with, "the Law of Attraction," so rigidly that they suggest we must control our thoughts and only think about the things we want in life so we can attract it to us. I am *partially* supportive of this theory. However, I cannot, in good conscious, subscribe to the idea that if we slip up and think a negative thought we are going to attract personal catastrophe in our life. I do agree that dwelling on negative thoughts certainly will attract more disharmony in our lives. Importantly, even if we are incredibly optimistic, our lives are intertwined with the lives of others. Other people have their own thought patterns and are attracting or creating a variety of circumstances into their lives. This being said, it is nearly impossible for us not to experience 'ripple-affect' repercussions of those whose lives interact with our own. In other words, we are mostly in control of the good or bad we attract into our lives with our own thoughts…but as the old saying goes, "stuff happens!" Sometimes situations and events are simply out of our control. What is always within our control is how we handle those situations once they are upon us.

Understanding the law of attraction

Our conscious thoughts soak into our subconscious mind. Our subconscious does not know the difference between reality and non-reality. So, if our thoughts are focused on lack, pain, worry, negativity, inability to achieve — that is the reality of your subconscious mind. If you have positive goals, thoughts or dreams for yourself, AND you continually support them by thinking about them, writing them down, telling others about them, and praying about them, you are far more likely to achieve what you desire. Meditate and visualize yourself living your dreams…by so doing, it becomes the reality of your subconscious and those dreams and goals may begin to manifest in your life.

The "Law of Attraction" is an interesting phenomenon. It may not work 100% of the time but it certainly works more than 50% of the time…meaning there is more to this philosophy than just 'chance.' So teach yourself – better yet — FORCE yourself to focus on the positive things you want and expect in life. Then take the ACTION STEPS necessary to make them happen. Regardless of the challenges you face, think more about the good things you want in your life and attract them to you. I am not saying it is easy, but it is a pattern that will bless your life and the lives of those around you, **abundantly**.

Thoughts lead to actions; actions can become habits;
habits change lives!

I have touched on thoughts and how they can affect outcomes or indirectly affect our health. Now let's take a look at how thoughts can, and do, directly affect our nervous system, thereby affecting our health.

Thoughts directly affect our physiology

One of the most primitive examples of this is called the "fight or flight" response. When we are startled, scared, or THINK we are in danger, it stimulates the sympathetic nervous system. The adrenal glands receive a message from the brain through the nerves and that innate intelligence says, "Emergency! Emergency! Release the Adrenaline!! " Blood vessels constrict, reducing blood flow, to the skin and digestive organs, while at the same time, dilating arteries to the muscles. This provides the necessary oxygenated blood to the muscles for defense or a quick escape. Muscles tense, pupils dilate, the heart races and respiration is increased all in a split second. Why? Because the sense of danger triggered a THOUGHT and the THOUGHT provoked the nervous system to stimulate a chemical release of epinephrine in the blood creating a physiological change. Stress triggers this response to a smaller degree. A simple daily example would be the following:

The other day Dave was driving to work. He noticed the traffic was backed up ahead. "Oh, no," he thinks, "I hope this does not make me late for work." Dave subconsciously tightened his grip on the steering wheel. His shoulders shrug a little. Traffic moved along at a snail's pace and he looked down at the clock. "Yep, this is going to make me late! I knew it!" He sighed to himself. Looking back up to the road he noticed he was rolling forward and traffic has stopped again. As he quickly applied more force to the brake pedal, he unknowingly tensed every muscle of his upper body and with a jerk of his car he came to a halt again. "Whew, that was close," he thought as he nearly rear-ended the car in front of him.

Now, the stress of traffic and the thought of being late had caused Dave to hold his shoulders in an elevated, tense position for some time. These muscles were pulling on bones causing misalignments of the spine that further affected his nervous system. The blood vessels to his head were affected causing a headache. The nerve supply that exits the spine between the 7th bone in the neck and the 1st bone in the mid-back were affected by these tight muscles in the neck and shoulders thus reducing the nerve flow to the heart and lungs. Dave doesn't feel this but these subluxations or misalignments of the spine left undetected and uncorrected can

22

lead to other problems such as his high blood pressure, numbness and tingling in the hands, migraines and difficulty sleeping.

Unfortunately, the 'fight or flight' response also has a suppressive effect on the immune system. Research has shown that we have more visual and auditory stimulus in four hours of one day than our grandparents had in three full months of their lives! The result is our nervous system is in a constant state of over-stimulus. Our 'fight or flight' mechanism is constantly engaged, at least to some degree, by input resulting in systemic inflammation and reduced immunity. Many of the diseases we face today are based on inflammation. This will be addressed later in more detail.

Stress, or thoughts that simulate negative emotions, affect the autonomic portion of our nervous system. This directly affects organ function. Another example would be stomach acid production. Because the stomach contains such a strong concentration of hydrochloric acid, it has GOBLET cells lining the inner wall to produce a protective mucus lining, acting as a shield between the destructive acid and the vulnerable stomach tissue. Stress causes an imbalanced neurological stimulation of the PARIETAL cells and the GOBLET cells which can result in higher acid production in conjunction with reduced mucus production leaving the stomach lining more susceptible to self-injury or ulcers.

Now we see how thoughts are a foundational part of OPTIMAL HEALTH. Thoughts affect everything from reducing pain to weight loss/weight control, to our immunity and how well we fight off infection or disease.

Understanding the profound effect our thoughts have will help emphasize the importance of forming habits to help program our thoughts DAILY for the POSITIVE.

Training ourselves in the way we think can help attract not only more of the 'positive things' we desire in life, but can also directly affect our health. Thoughts, when cultivated, become a desire. Desire can then serve as fuel for action. Actions shape habits. Proper habits help us achieve our health goals and much more.

According to my friend and author, David Putvin, "desire" is not a strong enough word for anything but a short-term goal; you have to be "passionate" about what you want.

Define your goals with passion

It is human nature to prioritize, on some level, every action we take throughout the day. Often times a desire, or action step, toward a goal is bumped by some other priority. For example: a planned time to exercise may be bumped by the need to take care of a sick child. If priority distractions of this kind happen often enough, we do not keep the habits necessary to accomplish our goals. This leads to discouragement, and finally loss of interest in the original goal.

All goals require some form of discipline, but certain goals we make will have a more deeply rooted importance to us. These are the goals we are *passionate* about. When you combine passion and discipline you are unstoppable. Why? Because these are the things from which even a priority detour can only temporarily distract you.

Some ways to 'stay on course' with your goals include anchoring goals to things you are passionate about. Daily rituals can help you avoid negativity, and can help refocus your passion to better leverage your goals to insure success.

Leverage your goals

This should be a "Technique for Advanced Living" in itself. Once an individual has the passion necessary to make a goal take flight it becomes much easier if the goal is "Leveraged." Humans are primarily driven to action by two things. Pleasure and Pain. Some individuals are pleasure driven meaning they do what needs to be done for the 'reward' of completion. Others do what need to be done primarily to avoid the 'pain' of what will happen if it is not done. Everyone is driven by these TWO motivators or a combination of the two. In order to maximize your big goals simply leverage them by using both tools to your advantage.

Example:

Mary wanted to lose 30 lbs. Her friend, Sally, told her it is a waste of money to buy a new outfit before she actually loses the weight. This is an example of zero leverage, only a hope and dream.

Later Mary was talking with another friend Mike about her conversation with Sally. Mike asked Mary, "What two things do you really want to give yourself as a reward when you reach your goal?" She replied, "I really do want a new outfit. I think I would like a new IPod to listen to music and audio books while I workout...well, I guess that doesn't count because I wouldn't really want to wait...I know, a trip to Cancun!"

"Great," Mike said, "Now this may sound strange but what are some of your least favorite things to do, for example, around the house or at work?"

Mary thought for a minute then replied, "I hate cleaning the bathroom, especially the toilet and at work filling drives me crazy."

"Perfect," exclaimed Mike. Mary looked at him quizzically. "Mary," Mike continued, "Here is what you do if you REALLY want to reach your goal."

First, you set a date or deadline for your goal and write it down.

Second, you need to leverage your goal with a reward that is equal in value to the task or goal at hand. In other words, you don't get a new Ferrari for cleaning your bedroom.

- The outfit and the IPod will work perfect. [PLEASURE LEVERAGE] Mary, you need to find the outfit you want in the size you want to fit when you reach your goal and YOU BUY IT. Then you pick out the IPod you really want, the style and color you are dreaming about and YOU BUY IT. You keep the IPOD in its box and leave it out in plain sight where it is under your nose every day. **You can't use it yet.** Same with the outfit or maybe even hang the outfit on the wall. A few small tack holes in the wall to hold up the outfit are worth the benefits, that way you see it every day.

Third, [PAIN LEVERAGE] you find a friend who would like the outfit and the IPod and you tell them about your goal. Let them know if you don't make or exceed your goal that YOUR "rewards" become a gift to THEM. (They will be cheering on some level but more likely teasing you not to make it which will hopefully push you harder to make your goal) Regardless the "rewards" are yours or theirs; they do not simply go back to the store. No returns, no exchanges.

Fourth, (In Mary's case, this is a good option) Set a half way goal. You get the IPod when you get half way. Let someone know to keep you accountable. Mary, you don't get it at 13 lbs not at 14lbs. Mary has to reach 15 lbs. But then Mary, your workouts for the second half of your goal should be much more fun. You can listen to your music or audio books. [PLEASURE LEVERAGE]

- Mary, offer to clean the toilets for one month at work or the homeless shelter. Otherwise, offer to do not only your filing at work but the filing of one or two co-workers if you do not make your goal. [PAIN LEVERAGE]

- Mary, there has to be accountability. Notice that both the loss of the PLEASURE ITEMS to someone who knows your goal and the PAIN of doing something you do not want to do involve other people…that equals [ACCOUNTABILITY]

Mary noticed her mouth was open during most of the suggestions made by Mike. She was a little scared at the commitment required to do what Mike was recommending but it all made perfect sense. She knew in her heart of hearts that if she leveraged her goal in the ways Mike was advocating she would be truly driven, by both pleasure and pain, to achieve her goal.

Change your thoughts

Here are some "Morning Rituals" to help lay the foundation for positive power thoughts through the day. Do these steps every day for 30 days and see what a difference it makes in your life! You will find yourself wanting to continue these steps as life-long habits.

TECHNIQUES FOR ADVANCED LIVING
THOUGHTS

Reduce stress, improve your immune system and attract what you want in life by changing some habits that will affect your thoughts in a POSITIVE way. Try starting your day with these morning rituals.

START YOUR DAY WITH GRATITUDE. Before you even leave your bedroom, give thanks to GOD for the wonderful things you enjoy: your family, your freedom, another day on this beautiful planet... whatever you are thankful for.

AVOID THE NEWS and the newspaper at least at the beginning of the day (and right before bed at night). There is much negative information in the news that YOU DON'T NEED floating around in your head all day. Many people start their day with who was robbed, killed, raped, or mutilated; what natural disaster happened; economy problems; and so on. Throughout the day we all begin to talk about the negative atrocities of the world, focusing on the wrong things with our co-workers. DON'T. It is absolutely counterproductive to your mental, spiritual, and physical well-being.

GIVE YOUR BRAIN POSITIVE BRAIN-FOOD FIRST THING IN THE MORNING. When avoiding the news and other negative info, you now have more time for POSITIVE INPUT. Start your day reading from the Scriptures. Just 10 to 30 minutes. If you are not a religious person, read or listen to a self-help book. Self-help books are great on MP3 or CD. You can listen to them while taking a morning run or working out.

EXERCISE. Get your heart pumping in the morning to circulate more fresh oxygenated blood to your brain and muscles. (Yes, this is a physical step and I will explain the physiological reasons for this later, but it is powerful in helping you have a great day every day). Like I said, listen to something motivational while you are exercising and you are 'killing two birds with one stone," on your morning rituals. A brisk walk or run is great. Go to the gym and hit the weights or play some racquetball. At minimum, do at least 50 pushups and 50 crunches every morning. If you can't do 50 straight, no problem, do 10 at a time and in a matter of weeks you will be able to do them all at once. There is a great website or app (www.hundredpushups.com) with a self-training program to get you up to 100 consecutive push-ups within 6 weeks.

MEDITATE. Take time (5 to 15 minutes per day) to clear your mind and simply think of NOTHING. I know, it sounds strange and it is actually quite difficult. The conscious mind is always thinking of something. "What's for dinner? Oh, I need to get to the bank today; I need to call 'so and so' to reschedule our lunch appointment." Clearing your mind, picturing a clear blue sky, or the waves gently crashing on a beach, whatever peaceful sight you prefer and trying to hold that thought while you breath in and out slowly and smoothly. It is powerfully calming and helps you fully charge your "mental batteries" for the day. One of the greatest tutors on the art of meditation is Dr. Deepok Chopra.

VISUALIZE. At the end of your meditation, visualize yourself doing the activities you want to do. Visualize or imagine yourself living the life you want to live. Visualize your day going exactly how you want it to.

- If you have a presentation today, picture yourself smiling, and presenting your information to your audience. Picture them participating in the way you want them to. Picture yourself connecting with that audience.

- If you have a date with your grandkids at the park, picture yourself walking with them on the grass, smiling and laughing together.

- As a doctor, each workday morning, I visualize my office full of happy satisfied patient families who are *wellness-educated* rather than focused on pain. I visualize those in pain smiling and feeling better.

Visualize what you want or expect to happen, and it will. "The thought precedes the action." When we visualize and prepare our thoughts for what we want, we are 10 times more likely to have those thoughts realized.

PLAN OUT YOUR DAY. Before you walk out the door to work or otherwise, make a plan. Write down a CHECKLIST of what you need to get done today so you don't forget anything. A Checklist really helps manage stress. The process should literally take less than 2 minutes. Simply having a checklist for the day will insure you won't forget important things, thus eliminating potential anxiety later in the day.

These techniques are fantastic habits or 'rituals' that help start each and every day on the right track, making the remainder of the day feel more organized, positive and productive. Remember, it takes 21 consecutive times to form a habit. I recommend you set a goal to do this for at least a month. Don't overwhelm yourself, take it one day at a time, then complete a week. After just one week you should notice a great difference that will keep you motivated to continue. Whatever you do, don't give up. If you slip up one day, just get back on track. Every action step you take to keep your headspace clear of "garbage" and full of positive self-improving thoughts is a step in the right direction!

REM and sleep cycles

You may be asking yourself, "When am I supposed to do all these things?" I already get up at 6A.M. and I have to be at work by 8A.M.

I would say, get up earlier.

Just doing what I have mentioned above is more important than the time you do them but I can tell you this; "Sleep is overrated," as my friend and mentor, Dr. CJ Mertz has said. We don't need sleep, per se, what we need is REM.

REM is 'rapid eye movement,' the 5th level or deepest stage of sleep. This stage is critically important because during REM:

- The body regenerates and recharges itself best, billions of cells are replaced or repaired during the REM Cycle

- The Nervous System repairs itself

- The body does the most healing and fighting of infections during the REM cycle

- Lack of REM can lead to mental instability (inability to think rationally)

- Lack of REM will begin to reduce our lifespan

Have you ever heard of the, "Military Sleep Deprivation Studies?" Soldiers who participated in this study were tested in an upscale cave where they had no sun light and no way to track time. Forced to stay awake for days, they began to literally go crazy. The soldiers became delusional! Interestingly, they began to take long slow blinks and would actually drop into REM for the few seconds when they closed their eyes.

The human body has many cycles that take place within it. There are digestive cycles, respiratory cycles, the menstrual cycle, and yes, sleep cycles. We can override them, or we can work with them and maximize our health and energy levels.

Apparently we are innately designed or programmed to get our best REM between 10pm and 12am. After that we experience intermittent moments of REM until about 3:30am. Once 3:30am has passed we usually are just 'sleeping.' Translation: we are just wasting time!

Research suggests we should develop regular sleep habits. One study demonstrated that going to bed the same time every night can enhance sleep quality. Two groups were asked to sleep 7.5 hours per night, one group on a regular schedule while the second varied their bedtime between 10pm and midnight. Subjects in the group that regulated their sleep patterns showed:

- Decreased daytime fatigue
- Greater and longer-lasting improvements in alertness
- Greater sleep efficiency. (They fell asleep faster and stayed asleep longer, and most importantly, through the night)[6]

Additional studies:

Other studies have shown it is not **quantity** of sleep we need but quality. Again, pointing to REM. A study group lowered their regular sleep hours from eight hours per night to five and continued over four consecutive nights followed by two recovery nights. The subjects experienced less S1 and S2 stages of sleep while S3 and S4 (REM) increased. Subjects reported their sleep quality improved.[7]

In fairness, different stages of life require more sleep. For example, a new born baby is growing at an exponential rate compared to the later years of life. Babies require a great deal of sleep because they are generating an enormous number of new cells.

When we are fighting a cold or infection we need more rest and more sleep (REM) to maximize healing, cell replacement and regeneration.

However, we usually do not need the amount of sleep we have been taught. Eight hours is excessive for most adults. Since what we really need is REM we can maximize REM while minimizing unnecessary sleep. This is done by setting a sleep schedule and sticking to it. Going to bed within 15 minutes of the same time each evening, preferably at or before 10pm is key, before midnight is essential. Schedule to wake up the same time each morning (between 4 and 5 a.m.). This sets your body in a rhythm or sleep pattern that will help your body establish a regulated sleep cycle naturally increasing your REM. You will find you can wake up at 4 a.m. or 4:30 a.m. and be wide awake ready for the day. When you hit the pillow at night (if you stay in pattern) you will find yourself dropping almost immediately into an S5 (REM) slumber. Seriously, you should be asleep within minutes! It is amazing.

So, if you simply do not have enough time in your day or can't seem to wake up early enough to exercise and do your morning, "Techniques for Advanced Living," then you do not believe in your own body cycles. Remember, you don't need sleep, you need REM.

I know it sound crazy. If you are a "night owl" who never goes to bed before midnight, it is clear that you are not getting enough REM and it will have a long-term effect on your health.

The "Graveyard" shift. It is called that for a reason. Statistically speaking, those who work graveyard for more than 10 years of their life typically have a life expectancy 10 years less than the national average. So, yes, robbing yourself of quality sleep or REM takes time off your life.

Other REM robbers:

- Eating just before bed
- Going to bed after midnight
- Caffeine
- Alcohol
- Tobacco
- Red Meat
- Dairy Products
- Carbonation
- Inactivity
- Inconsistent bed time
- Street Drugs
- Many Pharmaceutical Drugs

TECHNIQUES FOR ADVANCED LIVING

REM: Set up the habit of proper sleep cycles to maximize your REM. This will improve your energy levels, and add time to your life...literally. Not only is it healthy to increase REM and decrease "sleep" but if you are sleeping 8 hours per day and reduct it to 6 while still getting better rest and rejuvenation with improved sleep patterns...you just added 730 hours or an entire month of productive time to each year of your life!

What would you do with this added time to your life?

Exercise in the morning? Prepare healthier breakfasts? Write a book? Write down a couple of the things you want to do but keep telling yourself "I don't have the time." See what you can move around to fit them in the extra month you just discovered!

Footnotes:

4. As a Man Thinketh; Think and Grow Rich; The Secret; and many more

5. As a Man Thinketh; James Allen, 1902, Copyright 2006

6. R. Manber et al., "The Effects of Regularizing Sleep-Wake Schedules on Daytime Sleepiness," Sleep 19, no. 5 (June 1996): 432-41

7. Elmenhorst EM., "Partial sleep deprivation: Impact on the architecture and quality of sleep," Sleep Med. 2007, Oct 5

TRAUMA

TRAUMA COMES IN ALL SHAPES and sizes. From car accidents, slips or falls, sports injuries, or work-related injuries, to less noticeable repetitive micro-traumas like poor posture, improper ergonomics at your desk, poor sleeping position, etc. Often overlooked is our first trauma, the birth process. Particularly, if there is any pulling or twisting on the baby's head and neck it increases the chance of trauma. The use of forceps, vacuum extraction, and yes, even C-section deliveries, are traumatic enough to cause injury. (Please read the end-note on birth.)[8, 9, 10, 11, 12]

The lists of traumas we can experience are endless. Oft times, symptoms of a trauma go unnoticed for months or even years. WHEN WE HAVE A TRAUMA TO THE SPINE, NO MATTER HOW HARMLESS IT MAY SEEM, THE DEGENERATIVE PROCESS OR SPINAL DECAY IS ACCELERATED BY SIX TIMES.

Most people have the notion that osteoarthritis is just part of getting old. **It is not.** Now, there are some types of arthritis that are actually cyclic inflammatory diseases like rheumatoid arthritis.

However, typical arthritis, especially in the spine, is a much simpler and often preventable condition. Arthritis happens due to a trauma or repetitive micro-traumas, such as poor posture, sleeping on one's stomach, sitting at the computer all day without proper ergonomics, altered posture from carrying a heavy backpack full of books day in and day out, etc. These large or small traumas are what actually initiate the calcification process we call arthritis or degenerative joint disease. I have had 85-year-old patients with great spines (minimal traumas in life with good health habits) and I have seen countless younger individuals, even under the age of 40 with degenerated spines due to traumas such as car accidents, sports injuries, repetitive micro-traumas, etc. Stuff happens in life! It is not age, but rather lifestyle, or injuries combined with time (age), that leads to accelerated degeneration. This is one reason Chiropractic is such a powerful tool in preserving our health and longevity: it slows or stops the degenerative process by keeping proper movement and nutritional lubrication within joints reducing swelling and scar tissue formation.

Chiropractic is to the spine and nervous system what brushing and flossing is to our teeth.

It's simple. If we get a gaping cut in our skin, the body will lay down scar tissue to heal and stabilize the area. Scar tissue is not pretty. It is, however, much stronger than regular tissue but it lacks "function." Scar tissue does not stretch or respond as normal tissue does. If we get stitches for the gaping cut, there is minimal scar tissue. Yes, there still is some scaring, but the medical intervention of stitches helps the body to heal in a more "functional" way.

Likewise, when we have trauma to the spine or joints, the body recognizes the injured area is no longer stable, or is experiencing undue stress. It sends extra calcium to stabilize the hypermobile (unstable) or fixated (non-moving) joint. It is trying to lay down "bony scar tissue," or trauma-induced arthritis. Will it be stronger in the immediate area like other scar tissue? Perhaps. Will it lack normal function? Absolutely! In the spine, it will directly affect the nervous system, and therefore our health. Spinal joint or disc dysfunction affects the overall functional capacity of organs and tissues supplied by nerves at the specific spinal level involved. Ouch! That is why Chiropractic intervention, following a spinal trauma, or in conjunction with repetitive micro-traumas, is vital for the health and longevity of the spine. The health of the spine directly affects the nervous system and the overall health and longevity of the individual.

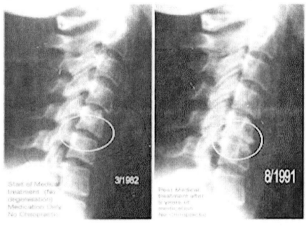

Trauma + Time = degeneration

Car accidents

Let's take car accidents, for example.[13] They are quite common in this day and age. Some are at high speeds and are seemingly more dangerous. Others are at low speeds (classified as less than 10 miles per hour), and commonly thought to result in little or no injury. Person "A" might say, "Whew, I was lucky. I totaled my car but I got away without a scratch." Person "B" might say, "Yea, this guy rear-ended me. It felt hard but there was no damage to my car, just a little scratch on the bumper. My neck muscles were tight for a couple of days but I am fine." Both individuals could be quite wrong regarding the extent of injury they received.

It is simple physics. Research by the San Diego Spinal Research Institute has shown that *statistically, more people are injured in low speed collisions than in high speed.* The San Diego Spinal Research Institute performed studies on live occupants who volunteered to sit in cars with sophisticated measuring devices attached to their bodies. During the study, other cars were strategically crashed into the occupied vehicle. The measuring devices calculated the force experienced by the body. They measured the *change in velocity* and the g's[14] the human body experienced when involved in a motor vehicle collision. The research is quite interesting. My colleagues found that even in a low speed collision[15] the head can momentarily experience over 13 G's or weigh 13 times its normal weight.

Modern cars are designed with "crumple zones." These zones absorb shock in a high speed impact. This is to reduce injury and save lives. Basically it reduces our "change in velocity" or DELTA V. The faster we change velocity the more g's placed on our body. It's the combination of a rapid change of velocity and increased g's experienced that injures us.

Case and point:

Imagine playing billiards. You set up a shot to hit the EIGHT BALL in the corner pocket. You aim and shoot the CUE BALL with a fair bit of force. Now it has become 'mass in motion'. Simply put, lets imagine the CUE BALL is moving at 30 miles per hour (velocity) in a straight line toward the EIGHT BALL.[16] At impact, the CUE BALL practically comes to a complete stop and the EIGHT BALL takes off like a rocket, straight ahead toward the corner pocket at just under 30 miles per hour. What just happened? The velocity was directly transferred to the EIGHT BALL. There was no resistance and no "crumple zone" to absorb the force (MASS x VELOCITY) so it was completely transferred to the EIGHT BALL. Thus, the EIGHT BALL went from zero miles per hour to almost 30 miles per hour in a fraction of a second! That huge change of velocity results in some serious g's[17] (Just for fun, imagine the EIGHT BALL being made of Nerf material and you can picture how differently the forces are transferred when there is absorption or a 'crumple zone.')

Now, imagine yourself in a car. Another vehicle with a mass of two tons hits you from behind at only 5 miles per hour. Let's say you are stopped on a flat surface **without** your foot **on** the brake. The other car (the bullet vehicle) impacts your car (the target vehicle). Your car jolts forward then you step on the brake. Your car went from 0 to just under 5 miles per hour in an instant. It was not enough to trigger the "crumple zone" and there is no visible damage to the vehicle. WHERE DID ALL THE FORCE GO? Answer: *Directly into YOU, the occupant.* You momentarily experienced g's roughly 8 to 10 times that of normal gravity. Meaning, for a split second, your 10-pound head weighed up to 10 times its normal gravitational weight or 100 lbs, while your body was in motion going from 0 to 5 miles per hour with the weight of 2 tons of force behind it!

Picture this in slow motion (or view it at www.shetlin.com):

1. Your car is suddenly pushed forward (faster than your reflexes or muscles can respond), your body, however, is pushed back into the seat. Your head, for a fraction of an instant, appears weightlessly suspended in mid-air, but with the increased g's applied, it now weighs over 100 lbs. Your poor neck is helplessly caught in the middle. The neck is made up of a few bones, several small muscles, ligaments, arteries, veins and, of course, the delicate spinal cord and brain stem. The neck is dangerously stretched between these forces.

2. Then directions change. The seat starts springing your body forward just as your head is catching up, in a rearward direction. The body is now catapulted forward while the head continues in a backward direction (often hyperextending over a head restraint that is set too low). The neck is dangerously stretched again.

3. The head begins to move forward as you finally firmly apply the brake. Even if you are not pressing on the brake, the seatbelt engages, bringing the torso to an abrupt stop while the head continues on a forward course. The neck is dangerously stretched again. All this in less than a second.[18]

There is much more to an acceleration/deceleration trauma or "whiplash," than I am discussing here but as you can see, even with a small accident, there can be harmful forces placed on the body. These forces may not fracture a bone, but can cause serious injury such as micro-tears in muscles, ligaments and tendons of the neck. Research shows that the body threshold for injury with *sheer* force is a mere 5 mph with a ligament failure rate of 100% likely at collision speeds of 8 mph.[19] A change in velocity of 5 mph is all it takes to increase the g's to be fast enough and hard enough to cause injury. Often times these are micro-traumas where the patient does not feel it right away.

I have seen countless patients who went to the ER to get checked after an auto accident (even minor ones) just for the peace of mind of getting a professional medical opinion. After a quick check, or even a set of x-rays or CT scan, the attending ER doctor tells them they are fine and sends them home with ice instructions, or a prescription for anti-inflammatory medication and muscle relaxants. Days, weeks or months later symptoms surface and they can't understand what caused them.

ER doctors are skilled physicians. But understand that they are looking for "emergency" conditions. Fractures, internal bleeding, brain injuries, immediate life-threatening problems. They are not looking for micro-tears of soft tissue, nerve impingement syndrome, subluxation, or the likes. These are difficult to find when you are not looking for them. So, by ER parameters, you may be fine, but that doesn't mean your spine and nervous system escaped the incident free and clear.

As an 18-year-old, I was involved in a car accident. Back in 1988 I was the proud owner of a 1965 Ford mustang. Baby blue, 90% restored and it ran great! One winter morning on the way to work, I slid down an icy road in a blizzard and had a head-on collision with a full-sized school bus. Blue Bird Bus Number 19, to be exact. Ouch! Needless to say, my car was totaled. My vehicle had low seat backs, therefore no head restraints. This, of course, did not help to reduce my injuries. Miraculously, I remained conscious and was able to walk away from the accident. I did sustain a mild concussion and it was recommended I have a medical check-up at the hospital. Off I went. After a short ride in an ambulance to the local hospital, I had a medical exam and a full set of spinal x-rays. The radiologist report stated, "No abnormalities noted, no fractures. I was released shortly

thereafter with a diagnosis of mild concussion and a skin lesion requiring 2 stitches. (I had actually split my left lower eye lid from the impact of my face on my own fist on the steering wheel. With all the force of Bus Number19 behind my fist, my poor eye didn't stand a chance).

Overall, I thought I had gotten out of the accident rather unscathed.

Following the accident, I soon noticed it was much more difficult for me to wake up early. My energy levels seemed lower somehow. At the gym I felt a general weakness. It was not until a full 6 weeks after the accident that symptoms of my 'undetected soft tissue injuries' really caught my attention.

During one of my morning workouts at the gym I was finishing with arm curls. It was a surprisingly low amount of weight because of the general fatigue I was experiencing. Suddenly, I felt a pain in my neck and my right arm went even weaker. I immediately left the gym.

Later that day I was at work when a co-worker noticed I was not quite right. I was rubbing my neck and had been guarding my right arm. He mentioned his dad was a Chiropractor and suggested I go see him at his office. I took his advice. After a thorough exam and x-rays he recommended I return the next day so he would have time to study my case appropriately before making his suggestions.

I had an appointment first thing the next morning and boy, was I glad.

The morning I was scheduled to return, I awoke and my right arm was completely useless. It had a 'sleepy' sensation and I couldn't seem to move it at all. My muscles were simply non-responsive. It was scary! I drove to the Chiropractic office, steering and shifting gears entirely with my left hand.

The doctor sat down with me and went over his findings from the exam and x-rays of the day before. He pointed out the severe loss of curve in my neck and a combination of other soft tissue injuries that had been there since the accident, but only recently reached a threshold to trigger these symptoms that brought me in. Now there was enough swelling in the joints to put pressure on the delicate nerves in the neck, affecting my right arm. He mentioned it would take time to heal and how I would benefit from Chiropractic, Physical Therapy and Massage.

I remember thinking to myself at the time, "How could the hospital say I had no significant findings when today I couldn't even use my arm?! Wouldn't they have seen the loss of curve or the misalignment of the bones in my neck?"

Regardless, the Chiropractor felt my neck and gave me a professional Chiropractic adjustment. I remember feeling as if a dimmer switch was slowly turned on from nothing to full power. A sense of energy flowed down my arm; within seconds I was able to move it again. The symptoms were relieved but I still had a lot of work to do to restore what I had lost (the curve in my neck) and to stabilize the tissues.

Now it is many years since that accident and as a Chiropractor myself, I can understand why the Emergency Room doctors were not looking for what this Chiropractor found. The doctors were doing their job, making sure there were no "immediate life-threatening" signs of trauma present such as, fractures, tumors, internal bleeding, etc. *Though Chiropractors look for these things too, our focus is in spotting misalignments, signs of micro-trauma, abnormal spinal curves, disc and joint spacing, and other problems that impact the nervous system in a negative way.* These symptoms are not any more difficult to spot than a fracture, but if you are not looking for them, they are easy to miss.

It is important to note that my case was an acute injury, and that it was treated early. Many people wait a long time before seeking Chiropractic care. This is tragic because the longer the problem exists, the longer it takes to fix it – if it is still correctable. It is not uncommon for a case to take a week, a month, or even longer before symptoms subside. In my case, I felt almost immediate relief. In spite of the improved symptoms, I was not done with rehabilitative care. I continued for some time, on a regular basis, restoring proper movement to the joints of my spine, and doing therapy to restore the curve in my neck, and stabilizing the torn soft tissues.

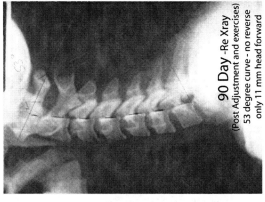

90 Day -Re Xray
(Post Adjustment and exercises)
53 degree curve - no reverse
only 11 mm head forward

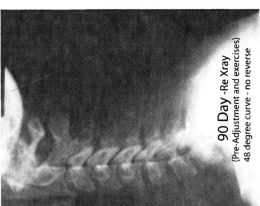

90 Day -Re Xray
(Pre-Adjustment and exercises)
48 degree curve - no reverse

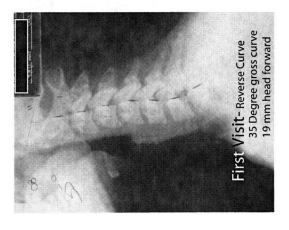

First Visit - Reverse Curve
35 Degree gross curve
19 mm head forward

Current patient with a case similar to my own

Remember that traumas come in all shapes and sizes, from repetitive micro-trauma like poor posture, bad sleeping position or poor ergonomics at work to more evident trauma like a broken bone or car accident. Trauma to organs can affect our health systemically or all over. Trauma to the spine affects our nervous system, which controls EVERYTHING in the body and therefore, can also affect our health systemically.[20]

Posture

Posture is a critical part of our health and well-being. Altered curves in the spine directly affect the nervous system, and thus our health. Many everyday activities result in repetitive micro-trauma: poor ergonomics while working at a computer; talking on the phone for long periods of time without a headset, keeping your head tilted at a bad angle for the duration; "Gameboy, PS3, Nintendo, DS, PSP" and other toys that keep kids' heads flexed down and forward; slouching; kids with heavy backpacks and poor posture to compensate for the load. These things seem so harmless but repeated, day after day, they negatively affect good posture.

"Better than 90% of the energy output of the brain is used in relating the physical body in its gravitational field. **The more mechanically distorted (poor posture, scoliosis, subluxations) a person is, the less energy available for thinking, metabolism and healing.**" ~*Dr. Roger Sperry, 1980 Nobel Prize for Brain Research*

Simply put, posture really is the window to the spine. The spine is the window to the nervous system. The nervous system controls EVERY cell, organ, muscle, gland, and hormone or chemical in our body, thus the spine really is the window to our health. Several studies referenced in this book support this fact.

Poor Posture   Good Posture   Poor Posture

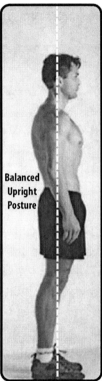

With poor posture habits, like "forward head carriage," a number of problems can develop. They may not show up immediately, but with time, one can develop chronic headaches, high blood pressure, numbness and tingling in the arms or hands, respiratory problems, and aesthetically, the dreaded "granny hump," to name a few. The mid-back will begin to compensate with an increased curve or "hump back." This can affect a number of organs. The low back will compensate with a loss of curve and stabilize itself with a shortened hamstring or a "sway back," meaning too much curve.

Loss of proper curve and joint function in the low back can affect digestive organs, reproductive organs, and even the body's ability to properly sense where your feet are. This impedes balance and equilibrium.

Scoliosis

Scoliosis is another form of altered curves in the spine and results are similar. Studies have shown that individuals with scoliosis typically have little or no ill effects early on due to their distorted spine. However, they are far more likely to have digestive and other chronic health problems later in life. They also have a life expectancy 10 years shorter than the average person.[21, 22, 23] (Wow, if an individual has scoliosis and is working graveyard shifts they are really burning the proverbial candle at both ends!) I have personally seen individuals with severe scoliosis and hyperkyphosis who have lived long lives with minimal health challenges. Statistics give us averages. There are always a few that throw off the "expected outcome," just as George Burns didn't fit the statistics of longevity for smokers and drinkers.

The point with poor posture and altered curves in the spine is that the effects may not show up for some time, but in most cases, these health problems are completely preventable. Once altered curves are set in place, it takes a great deal of time to correct the distortion and oft times are NOT 100% correctable.

New research conducted by six medical doctors states, "For every millimeter our posture is shifted forward (anterior head carriage or an increased thoracic curve) we are far more likely to have chronic pain or chronic problems." Chronic problems mean headaches, immune challenges, digestive problems, etc.

Chiropractors have been reporting this for decades!

Everyone benefits from regular Chiropractic care to maximize the function of their spine and nervous system. But for individuals with scoliosis, regular Chiropractic care is ten times more essential. As Dr. Sperry said, "…The more mechanically distorted (poor posture, scoliosis, subluxations) a person is, the less energy is available for thinking, metabolism and healing." Taking care of our spine, and thus our nervous system, is vital for optimal health, improved quality of life, and longevity.

Trauma, when not treated with proper rehabilitation, leads to excessive scar tissue. Scar tissue in the spine can lead to early degeneration (arthritis) that will affect the nervous system and a number of "target tissues" in the body.

TECHNIQUE FOR ADVANCED LIVING

Avoid Injury: Of course, we try to avoid injuries such as falling off a roof or being in a car accident. Car accidents are just that… accidents…the unexpected.

Don't Delay Treatment After An Injury:

If you are involved in a car accident GET CHECKED BY A CERTIFIED SPECIALIST and get treatment to rehabilitate your body correctly thus minimizing long-term injury and expense.

Other injuries such as slips, falls, or sports injuries… rehabilitate them correctly or they lead to unnecessary or excessive scar tissue build-up and arthritis.

For all you "weekend-warriors," I hope you take this to heart. "An ounce of prevention is worth a pound of cure" so stretch, exercise, and warm-up before you play sports hero.

Professional athletes…train properly, stretch, and listen to your body. Sports like football, boxing, ultimate fighting, rugby, lacrosse and other impact sports can expose your body to repetitive micro-traumas or the occasional good hit which is no less damaging than a whiplash in a car. Don't play tough-guy and brush off impact injuries. See a Sports Chiropractor to maximize your performance and help minimize injury.

Footnotes:

8, 9, 10, 11, 12

The Human race has been delivering babies for thousands or millions of years (depending on your philosophical views). We have done this naturally for all but the last 100 years or so. It has only been in the most recent century that man has become so cocky as to believe this natural process is to be treated as a disease. The mother is at risk and needs to be hospitalized under doctor and nurse supervision in a sterile and impersonal environment. Fear tactics have been used where mothers are now terrified to deliver a baby outside of a hospital.

Why the fear? When we study other mammals they birth their young without a hospital, without power tools and without all the drama. Is labor and delivery risky? Yes. Is it difficult? Yes. Does it hurt? My wife tells me, yes! But is it a natural and self-perpetuating process? Absolutely! 99% of the time it does not require tools or doctor intervention.

After 9 months the perfect little body is ready to enter the world. Mom can actively participate or not. Even a pregnant paraplegic woman stranded on an island alone could deliver a baby without assistance in most cases. Sounds extreme, I know. The point I am trying to make is that the uterus muscle wants to push that baby out when the time is right. That is its job. Whether the mom, a nurse or doctors are actively trying to help, innate intelligence and the uterus will do their job.

In the 40's and 50's they used to knock mom out with drugs and when she woke up she had a new little baby. She was not even consciously involved in the process.

Today it is a scary and rushed event. Stakes are high for both mom and doctor. Mom is scared about the overall event, all the risk possibilities, and she thinks she has to have the baby in a hospital with a doctor. The cord could wrap around the neck, it could be breach, and we may need to perform an emergency C-section. The doctor is scared because the overhead cost for staff and hospital use is so high. The doctor may think, "We may need to do an emergency C-section, allowing me to charge more to meet my overhead." Not only that, if everything doesn't go perfectly, the mom might sue, so malpractice insurance is a must. This medical insurance is the 2nd most expensive in the industry. All this technology and protocol, yet America has one of the highest newborn mortality rates in the world. You would think we would have the lowest, but we don't!

How did we evolve, or devolve, to having this natural and beautiful process become so scary and mechanical?

History:

Natural birth happened for thousands of years. Midwives were the most common assistants. Why the boiled water and towels? To keep things clean minimizing infectious agents from being transmitted to mother and child. Midwives would apprentice with each other. They were patient and had ample experience in this one area.

Doctors came on the scene and started assisting in deliveries. [Doctors currently have a lot of schooling. However, when the medical profession was young, the pupil would simply follow another doctor around for a few months as an apprentice. Soon, the apprentice would start his own practice. In the 1800's they started schools requiring about 6 months of education.]

Doctors didn't know much about microorganisms. The physician, wearing an apron during delivery, would wipe blood and fecal matter on it, touching mom and baby many times, Oft times aprons were not washed well to show the 'experience' of the doctor. "See, I have performed numerous deliveries." No wonder moms and babies would get sick and die shortly after delivery.

In the 1800's, and with the invention of the microscope, we discovered these little microorganisms and began washing hands between patients and sterilizing things better. Soon we built sterile environments known as hospitals (sadly, they are not as sterile as we would like to believe).

Nowadays we are taught to think, "Having a baby anywhere but at the hospital is crazy. It is clean, staffed and has all the tools necessary. It is simply too risky to have a baby elsewhere." – At least that is what they want you to think.

[My Undergrad studies were at the University of Utah where I also worked at the hospital. I was in the OB/GYN

54

research division. I worked there for 2½ years before going to Chiropractic school. I have witnessed many deliveries and delivered three of my own children with the help of midwives. The credit, of course, goes to my wife Shannon who actually delivered our four children and did each in a different way.]

13. See www.shetlin.com for more information and videos.

14. The measurement of acceleration (or deceleration) in units of gravity on Earth's surface.

15. Collisions under 10 miles per hour.

16. *Mass + Velocity = Force*

17. Also important to note the cue ball and the eight ball are of near equal mass. The cue ball went from 30 mph to near 0 mph in an instant. So, it experienced almost exactly the same change of velocity and g's.

18. Additional information from Dr. Shetlin's "Auto Accident Physics 101" Lecture DVD or visit Shetlin.com for more video footage.

19. Anterior longitudinal ligament injuries in whiplash may lead to cervical instability. Medical engineering & physics 2006; 28:515-524 Stemper BD, Yohanandan N, Pintar FA, Rao RD

20. Sympathetic Segmental Disturbances: The evidences of the associated, in dissected cadavers, of visceral disease with vertebral deformities of the same sympathetic segments. Henry Winsor, MD; Medical Times, November 921, pp 1-7

21. The effect of myofascial release (MFR) on an adult with idiopathic scoliosis. LeBauer A, Brtalik R, Stowe K., J Bodyw Mov Ther. 2008 Oct;12(4):356-63. Epub 2008 Jun 4

22. Conservative management of neuromuscular scoliosis: personal experience and review of literature. Kotwicki T, Jozwiak M.,Disabil Rehabil. 2008;30(10):792-8. Review.

23. The impact of positive sagital balance in adult spinal deformity, SPINE; September 15, 2005:30(18) 2024-9 Glassman SD, Bridwell K, Dimar Jr, Horton W, Berven S, Schwab F. (all MDs)

PREVENTION AND EXERCISE

IT IS NO SURPRISE THAT the *more physically fit* we become the less likely we are to sustain injury in the day-to-day rigors of life. Should we sustain an injury from trauma while we are physically fit, the recovery from that injury is much quicker. Granted, there are some injuries that fall outside the realm being discussed here such as a severe head injury or an amputation. Working out at the gym for three years prior to sustaining one of those kinds of injury is not necessarily going to help speed up a person's recovery. However... Exercise in itself is an interesting human physique anomaly. We just talked about "micro-traumas" and how bad they can be; causing soft tissue injuries that lead to scar tissue and potential long term health challenges. Yet we are also talking about exercise which is really a controlled set of micro-traumas to muscle and supporting tissue. Exercising the human body, when done properly, leads to the buildup, or replacement, of damaged muscle cells with bigger and stronger muscle cells. Anaerobic exercise such as weight lifting can increase the size or mass of muscle usually with quick-powerful muscle cells. Aerobic exercises such as running and biking typically generate strong endurance type muscle cells. The irony of each of these activities is the process of micro-trauma leading to improved physique and fitness.

There is good micro-trauma and bad micro-trauma. When we exercise properly we stimulate muscle growth. As former Mr. Universe / Mr. America / Mr. Olympia, Larry Scott, once told me, "Muscle is the furnace that burns fat." As we increase our muscle mass we increase our ability to more readily get rid of unwanted fat.

So there is a balance. Some people prefer exercise that is body sculpting such as weight lifting and have no interest in cardiovascular workouts. Others don't like weights and prefer only to do aerobic exercise such as dancing, biking, running or jogging. I can tell you this, those that exercise and still struggle with their weight or physique should try cross-training so each week they are doing a little of both aerobic and anaerobic exercise.

To those individuals who are completely inactive, all I can say is, "Motion is LIFE." Your body needs movement. Exercise, on some level, is necessary on a daily basis. In most countries the average individual walks over 8 miles per day. The average American walks less than 1.5 miles per day. A short brisk walk, or a few sit-ups and push-ups DAILY are great ways to get the blood circulating and tell your body you want to get it moving again.

When perform aerobic exercise we are: 1. burning calories; 2. exercising our cardiovascular system; and 3. mildly increasing our metabolism.

As we performing weight training exercises we are simulating muscle growth. Don't worry ladies — you won't bulk up like a guy because you exercise. Why? Because, ladies, you lack the hormone Testosterone which is necessary for muscles to "bulk up" like men. However, you will tone up beautifully and greatly increase your metabolism. A side benefit is having more liberty to eat what you want without weight gain. Guys, you will bulk up some and also find that you are simply burning more calories through the day with less effort.

Cross-training creates a more balanced physique and increases your, "fat burning furnace," by giving you more muscle mass. This, as I mentioned, gives you more leeway in what you can get away with eating without such brutal consequences or roller-coaster physique changes. However, once you are looking and feeling better it is normal to desire to eat healthier food. It becomes a health perpetuating cycle. One of the best books I have read on balancing these exercises, physique reshaping, and eating better is, "Body for Life," by Bill Phillips.[24] Another good one is, "Burn the Fat, Feed the Muscle," by Tom Venuto.[25]

"Okay, Dr. Shetlin, so cross training is a good thing. How do we best implement these exercises to maximize improving our health and minimize our likelihood of injury?"

We talked about alternating between cardio/aerobic exercises and anaerobic/weight lifting. Obviously some exercise is better than none and exercise anytime of the day is better than no exercise at all. HOWEVER, there are times in the day to exercise that will yield a greater result with less effort than others.

Jared Wash, author, certified personal trainer, nutritionist, and online fitness coach, says that a cardio workout in the morning before breakfast burns THREE times the amount of fat as compared to a workout later in the day. According to Larry Scott and his research team in Japan, exercising first thing in the morning is 300% more effective than later in the day. Three times and 300% are pretty much the same, either way you look at it. Exercise in the morning has a significant advantage over working out later in the day.

According to their findings, when we exercise (either aerobic or anaerobic) in the morning before breakfast, while we are still in a "fasting" state, the body releases a greater amount of human growth hormone. In actuality, it creates more DHEA which creates more human growth hormone. This is important to understand because several nutra-ceutical companies produce and push ingestible products of hGH.[26] My understanding is that it is not effective to simply eat it; your body needs to produce it on its own for it to be helpful in increasing muscle mass and affecting metabolism. So, whatever we can do to naturally increase DHEA (which we will talk about more in the next section) and thus stimulate increased hGH will increase muscle mass and strength, as well as increase our metabolism or fat burning capacity.

Exercise is important, not simply for weight control, but for a vast number of other reasons. In modern society our intellect is stimulated more frequently, yet our bodies are challenged less and less, and life gets out-of-balance.

As previously referenced, we receive as much visual and auditory stimuli in 4 hours of our modern urban lifestyle than our grandparents received in an entire quarter of a year. Imagine that, our brain downloads and processes in 4 hours what our grandparents did in 3 months! Driving down the road there are signs to read, disc-jockeys and music from the radio, turn signals, billboards, flashing lights; then there is TV, news, commercials, newspapers, fast food menus, and drive-through restaurants. Constant mental input (both conscious and subconscious) while our body is barely moving.

We "urbanites" no longer farm, lift, carry, saw, pull, load or exert on a daily basis to keep us fit…we now have machines to do that for us. Today, forcing ourselves to exercise, lift, push or run is critical to maintaining a healthy lifestyle.

How important is exercise on the global aspect of our body and health?

Off the charts!

- Exercise increases metabolism, as we already discussed.
- Exercise increases blood flow to ALL tissues.
  - Increased blood flow increases oxygen delivery to tissues. So exercise increases oxygen delivery to all

tissues. (Cancer is an interesting thing to mention here because cancer cells can grow in a low-oxygen environment but healthy cells need to receive the required O_2 in order to survive and thrive.)

- Exercise burns calories and helps burn fat.
- Exercise challenges muscles causing them to grow.
- By challenging the muscles, which attach to the bones, exercise stimulates bone tissue to respond by up-taking more calcium from the blood thereby strengthening bones and reducing the occurrence of osteoporosis.
- Increased blood flow from exercise flushes the tissues, expelling toxins. This flushing of the tissues under greater pressure moves things along the lymphatic system (the body's sewer system).
- Exercise usually creates an appetite for healthier foods. Your body begins craving more of what it NEEDS.
- Exercise, done regularly, creates good habits so you want to continue exercising.
- Exercise creates the production and release of chemicals in the body that help you stay more alert through the day.
- Exercise helps you sleep better and deeper (level IV or REM).
- As exercise helps improve your sleep, you heal better and fight off infection more effectively.
- Better exercise and sleep stimulates more production of DHEA and thus HGH, which increases longevity, energy, and youthful vitality.
- Exercise helps fight cardiovascular disease.
- Exercise improves sex drive and performance.

These are just a few great reasons to exercise. Exercise is important at every age!

TECHNIQUE FOR ADVANCED LIVING

Exercise: Exercise is a staple of modern life. We have become a technological society. With these advancements many of us are less physically active in our day to day life. Exercise is essential.

ONE: Maximize your workout efforts by knowing what exercise is best for you and WHAT TIME will give you the best results fastest.

If you are healthy and just on maintenance workouts, any time is fine.

If you are trying to lose weight or bulk up some muscle mass, early morning is best.

TWO: Find your motivation and be passionate about keeping with it to form habits.

THREE: Sign up for events so you have goals to shoot for. Try a Fitness contest, Triathlon,

5K run, 10Krun or Marathon. Sign up and train for a Century bike ride.

Have a workout buddy if possible. This gives you some accountability.

FOUR: Journal your workouts. Keep a log of what you are doing and how it makes you feel.

*At Minimum: work up to 50 push-ups per day 6 days a week. Start out with 5 or 10 at a time.

Add in 50 abdominal crunches and a few chin-ups.

(This would be a 1 to 5 minute workout...who doesn't have time for that?)

Footnotes:

24. http://bodyforlife.com

25. http://www.burnthefat.com

26. DHEA (dehydroepiandrosterone) "DHEA contributes to more than 150 different metabolic functions. As such, it is the most comprehensive anabolic influence in the human biochemistry. Stress reduces DHEA levels. Low DHEA is associated with impaired immunity, rising cholesterol, increased risk for cancer and cardiovascular disease (America's first and second leading cause of death), low energy, declining sex drive, accumulation of excess fat, depression and memory loss." - The Metabolic Plan, Stephen Cherniske, M.S., 2003

CHASING THE CURE

Nutrition will be addressed in the next section, however combining a properly functioning nervous system, exercise, eating better and avoiding toxins, we can actually PREVENT most diseases. Let me say that again. The majority of diseases mankind faces are PREVENTABLE. Isn't that a novel idea? Rather than all the suffering, decreased quality of life, early loss of life and the ridiculous amount of money we spend each year looking for a "CURE" for diseases…how much better would it be if we changed our paradigm to a more affordable approach…

Finally, a cure for disease: Prevention!

Preventable diseases:

Cardiovascular disease*

- Heart attacks*
- High cholesterol / clogged arteries*
- High Blood pressure*
- Erectile Dysfunction*
- Strokes

- Obesity* – and the numerous health challenges secondary to it.
- Type II Diabetes* – and the numerous health challenges secondary to it.
- Cancer – in most cases. (How often do you hear of a vegetarian with colon cancer?)[27]
- AIDS – in most cases.

If we, as a country, or as a planet for that matter, spent less time and money [28, 29] on "Research for Cures," and focused more on PREVENTION, the world as we know it would have a pivotal proactive health shift. Unfortunately, we label something a disease then chase our tail searching for a cure...pill manufacturing, injections or vaccines, blind studies, double-blind studies, placebo studies and emergency crisis care for these diseases. PREVENTION IS THE CURE to the diseases listed above.

Ponder this. Cardiovascular disease, cancer, and complications from diabetes are three of the top four killers in America and rapidly growing around the world as others adopt our poor habits and import our unhealthy food products (cola, diet drinks, fast food restaurants, etc.).

The 5th leading killer in America is the medications we take to placate our symptoms for these and other ailments.

I am not against medication when used sparingly, but when I see patients enter my office taking 8 to 23 different prescriptions per day it begs the question, "Why?" Over 200,000 people in America die per year from the right prescription for the right diagnosis. [30, 31, 32] Many patients, who initially come to me, are on one medication for their primary condition, then taking a second and third medication to treat the side-effects of the first. Why would we want to complicate matters by having multiple prescriptions, all of which have their own side-effects?

64

Effect vs. side-effect

Our body is a complex micro-universe with its own pharmacy. As we ingest man-made chemicals to cause an *effect* or desired result, there will always be collateral damage of some kind. We usually call it a "side-effect." Bruce H. Lipton, PhD explains in his book, "The Biology of Belief" how there really is no such thing as a side-effect, just effect. We often look at a situation in simple, linear, or "Newtonian" logic. If we knock over domino "A," it will knock over domino "B", and so on. With this kind of thinking we can predict the outcome. However, our biology is much more complicated than that resulting in non-linear cause-and-effect, often referred to as a quantum or a cascade effect.

$$A \rightarrow B \rightarrow C \rightarrow D \rightarrow E \rightarrow F$$

Newtonian–Linear

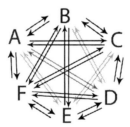

Quantum - Holistic

Understanding how this cascade effect works in the body it becomes clear that when we take a man-made medication it affects much more than we may realize. The common result is 'side'-effects.

Even the simplest medication such as Tylenol® taken for a headache has widespread effects. This non-steroidal anti-inflammatory (NSAID) cannot target the headache directly. It thins the blood throughout the body thus lowering the arterial pressure and at times alleviating the headache. However, tissues are affected throughout the body. Liver and kidneys have to deal with the toxic byproducts of the drug. There are unhealthy byproducts that are never flushed from the system, but accumulate in the kidneys over a lifetime.

Research shows that NSAIDS, though they alleviate headaches, as well as pain and joint swelling, are inflammatory to the cardiovascular system increasing the chance of heart attack by up to 5 times.

Remember the heavily marketed anti-inflammatory pain reliever, Vioxx,® At the time it hit the market, it was promoted more than any drug to date. With the help of TV and radio it quickly became the popular NSAID of choice. Then, to everyone's surprise, people started dying of heart attacks left and right. Come to find out, Vioxx helped reduced joint swelling and pain but increased cardiovascular inflammation nearly 10 times!

People using Vioxx were far more susceptible to having a heart attack, especially in the first 2 weeks of use.[33]

More than 26,000 Americans died within a year from cardiovascular problems secondary to the use of Vioxx to reduce joint pain.

Please listen to your innate intelligence rather than the television as to what you need and what is healthy for you. Eating more fruits and vegetables (non-inflammatory foods), and using food supplements, if necessary. Additionally, exercise can do a lot more for an individual than remaining over-weight and taking an aspirin a day to "prevent the risk of heart attack." Aspirin, as we just discussed, is a NSAID so it does cause a thinning of the blood, thus reducing blood pressure to a degree. However, it is INFLAMMATORY to the cardiovascular system, actually increasing the risk of heart attack.

You might think, "Wait a minute, the TV and my doctor tell me to take ½ of an aspirin or a baby aspirin every day to help prevent a heart attack." Thanks to a great marketing campaign that is what millions of people think. I can tell you this, headaches and heart attacks are not due to a lack of aspirin in your blood.

There are so many natural things we can do and health promoting products we can take, without side-effects that advance our natural health, healing and disease prevention. However, we must avoid the toxins and poisons marketed to us as acceptable or even beneficial to our body. It seems in this day and age, information is readily accessible, but knowing truth from fiction regarding health is a challenge. Once we know the truth, implementing it to our personal benefit is our responsibility.

TECHNIQUE FOR ADVANCED LIVING

Educate before you Medicate: Every man-made medicine will cause what we call commonly 'side-effects.' Before you take pills and potions, research alternative methods (herbs, dietary changes, exercise, chiropractic, acupuncture) to see if you have options without side-effects.

Before you take a drug:

1. Know the side-effects

2. Know what foods or drugs it reacts with

3. Know how long you will need to take it

4. Know the long term effects of taking that drug

Remember, "An ounce of prevention is worth a pound of CURE!" ~*Benjamin Franklin*

Footnotes:

27. http://www.health.harvard.edu/blog/vegetarian-diet-linked-to-lower-colon-cancer-risk-201503117785 "Those with a vegetarian diet are 23% less likely to develop colon cancer. Vegetarian who also eat fish are 43% less likely to develop colon cancer."

28. US disease research spending in millions / disease - http://report.nih.gov/rcdc/categories

29. $2.5 Billion US/year for just 3 diseases- http://www.globalnetwork.org/press/2009/2/4/how-much-world-spending-neglected-disease-reserch-and-development

30. The JOURNAL of the AMERICAN MEDICAL ASSOCIATION (JAMA) Vol 284, No 4, July 26th, 2000 article written by Dr. Barbra Starfield, MD, MPH, of the Johns Hopkins School of Hygiene and Public Health, shows that medical errors may be the third leading cause of death in the United States

31. American Journal of Medicine, July 1998

    "It has been estimated conservatively that 16,500 NSAID-related deaths occur among patients with Rheumatoid arthritis or Osteoarthritis every year in the United States.

32. New England Journal of Medicine

    The Food and Drug Administration suggests even higher figures, estimating NSAID use accounts for 10,000 to 20,000 deaths per year in the United States alone

33. Science Daily (May 3, 2006)

HARRISON • PART II

Shannon and I had a big decision to make. Actually, it was an easy decision, but the repercussions would have to be dealt with later on.

I understood there are 24 strains of bacteria that can cause meningitis, 8 of which are deadly. This little guy was in a fight for his life. I knew surviving meningitis without modern intervention was slim to none. Unfortunately, our medical hero was a series of the strongest antibiotics available and they have pretty scary side effects.

We did what any parents would do…save his life now, deal with the residual effects later.

Harrison was wheeled away to the ICU where he would receive his first of four daily intravenous doses of antibiotics. He was scheduled to receive another four every day for the next 21 days.

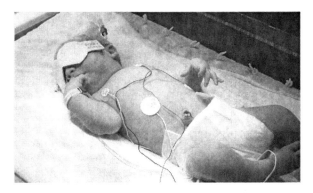

As I read the label on the antibiotics I mentally braced myself for the battle ahead. Should little Harrison survive, he would most likely be plagued with one of the following:

Possible side-effects include:

- Permanent hearing loss or deafness
- Permanent kidney problems
- Permanent motor-neurological problems (Cerebral-palsy)"

Trusting in modern medicine and putting our faith in the power of prayer, we took one day at a time. After a week in the hospital we were allowed to bring Harrison home to finish his antibiotic regimen. By the end of the month, the family was overjoyed to still have the latest addition to hold in our arms.

As time passed, I noticed a few "oddities" with our little one. He seemed 'floppy' and his eyes were always rolled up in his head. By the 2nd month he was ready for a pediatric check-up. After the exam, our pediatrician postured for the firm but sympathetic delivery of his findings. He said, "Jay, you and Shannon are going to have to prepare yourselves because this little guy is going to have some challenges. It looks like he has a serious case of cerebral palsy."

He said, "Harrison will be smart, but he will lack motor

coordination. Walking will be difficult, stairs even more so. He will likely never run or kick a ball." I could tell it wasn't easy for him to give us the news; it was even harder for Shannon and me to fight back the tears.

Driving home I realized that for the past two months I had been this child's dad but not his doctor. I was too close to the situation and had taken off my 'doctor hat' for the entire time. I had not adjusted him once since the day he entered the hospital.

As my mind raced through the steps I, personally, could take to help my son have a chance at a 'normal' childhood, an impression came to me. I knew what to do. I just needed to do it, believe in it, and be patient. The rest would take care of itself.

I decided right then I would be adjusting Harrison three times per week for six weeks, then two times per week for six weeks, then once a week for as long as it took. I would monitor his diet (after breast feeding) to make sure he received good nutrients and take steps to keep all toxins out. In other words, avoid junk food, candy, vaccines and other toxins that could hamper his already challenged nerve and motor development. For now, we needed to make sure mom was eating right since he was breast feeding.

Upon arriving home, I adjusted Harrison's neck with the gentlest of Chiropractic treatments. And to my amazement his eyes immediately began to track on objects. Now, in the neurologic world that, in itself, is nothing shy of miraculous!

He was still floppy and well behind in motor skill development. In the months that followed we continued to pray constantly. I treated him with Chiropractic, he had physical therapy with a specialist, we made sure he received good nutrition, and we kept the junk (toxins) out…

TOXINS

This section requires some clear definitions. As we have already discussed, to maximize our health and healing, we need the correct blueprints, a properly functioning nervous system, and the right nutritional substance. We are generating 300 billion new cells per day to replace dying cells. Without blueprints and nutritional building blocks, we wage a losing battle against poor health, disease and premature death. Getting the right things IN our body is vital. Equally important is keeping the wrong things OUT. Things that damage tissues, retard healing and accelerate disease and death are toxins. Toxins come in many shapes and sizes.

Toxin: "One of a number of poisons produced by certain plants, animals, and bacteria."

The term "toxin" is frequently used to refer specifically to a particular protein produced by some higher plants, animals and pathogenic (disease-causing) bacteria. A toxin typically has a high molecular weight (as compared to a simple chemical poison), is antigenic (elicits an antibody response), and is highly poisonous to living creatures.

*In the context of biology, **poisons** are substances that can cause injury, illness or death to organisms, usually by chemical reaction or other activity on the molecular scale, when a sufficient quantity is present.*

In medicine (particularly veterinary) and zoology, a poison is often distinguished from venom. Venom is usually defined as a biologic toxin that is injected to cause its effect, while poisons are generally defined as substances which are absorbed through epithelial lining such as the skin or gut.[34]

Therefore, a toxin or poison is anything put ON or INTO the body which can have an adverse affect such as injury, illness or death.

There are many toxins in our day-to-day life, affecting us in a negative manner, which we simply fail to recognize or take seriously. Too much of a good thing can become toxic. Sugar is a good example. Some vitamins are another example: Fat soluble vitamins are good for you, but in excess, can be toxic. Direct toxins include pollution in the air we breathe, chlorine or fluoride in the water we drink, harmful chemicals in the processed foods we eat, pesticides on the fruits we buy at the grocery store; antibiotics, free radicals, steroids and poisons in the meat we eat, and the list goes on. Prescription and over-the-counter drugs are, in fact, toxic to our bodies! For every symptom we try to affect with a drug, there are lists of "side" or adverse-effects from that drug. Author, Kevin Trudeau, in his book "Natural Cures They Don't Want You to Know About" cites numerous natural remedies for health ailments that are kept out of the public eye so drug companies can make billions of dollars off the promotion and use of their patented man-made chemicals with their numerous side-effects.

Pollutants

Exercise done early in the morning is more beneficial than later in the day particularly when it comes to pollution. The air is cleaner early in the morning, and when we are exerting ourselves and breathing heavily, we want the least amount of pollutants entering our lungs as possible.

Chemicals

These are found in everything, including the food we buy at the grocery store. This is a topic for another book in itself. If you read the labels on processed food, there are countless words that are difficult to spell and impossible to pronounce, describing what is being used in your food as molecular glue or preservatives. Even the fresh produce is sprayed with so many chemicals at the farm that they become hazardous to eat, especially without rinsing thoroughly.

Free radicals (Not a Toxin)

Free radicals are atoms or molecules in your body with an *unpaired electron*, making them highly unstable. Because electrons normally come in pairs, the free radicals collide with other molecules in an attempt to steal an electron, and may start a chain reaction, damaging your DNA and cells. Emerging science suggests this free radical damage may be linked to disease. Free radical scavengers, or antioxidants, bind with the free radicals before they can do their damage. We are exposed to free radicals by certain foods we eat; breathing in air pollutants, x-ray exposure from the sun and medical imaging, cell phone radiation, etc. We even create them ourselves with excretion and exercise. We encounter or create tens of thousands of free radicals each day. They are an unavoidable 'toxin' but they are easy to deal with.

Anti-oxidants

Free radicals are neutralized by "anti-oxidants." Anti-oxidants are molecules that have an *extra electron* that they can 'donate' to a free radical molecule, thus stabilizing the unstable molecule without becoming unstable itself.

The best source of anti-oxidants is in our daily diet. Fruits and vegetables are extremely important for receiving the anti-oxidants we require. If we are not getting 10 to 12 servings of fruits and vegetables per day, we are losing the battle. Unfortunately, most of us do not eat near enough fruits and vegetables. For this reason, supplements have become increasingly important in modern society. Scientific rumors are proving true with soil nutrient depletion where we need three of today's apples to equal the nutrients of a single apple in 1940.

Antibiotics

Antibiotics are a wonderful scientific discovery and are quite helpful in extreme illnesses. However, the use of antibiotics needs to be carefully considered before administering. Using antibiotics for a fever or simple ear infection often causes more harm than good.

Within our body we have an innumerable amount of "normal flora" or healthy bacteria that help our body with everything from digesting to immunity. Antibiotics are just that, "anti"- against "bio"-life. Antibiotics cannot distinguish between good bacteria and bad bacteria; it just kills everything in its path, including our good bacteria.

This affects our own immunity making us more susceptible to further infection. One, because we have lost part or all of our army of normal flora, and two, since our body did not fight the fight itself, true IMMUNITY was not gained. The antibiotics fought the fight for our immune system.

Antibiotics are great for life threatening infections, but be cautious in the overuse of them. The sniffles and ear infections are rarely reason enough for using antibiotics.

Pharmacological medication

Where do drugs come from? Generally speaking, a natural product is taken with a component that gives a desired effect. This active ingredient is titrated down to concentrate that specific component, thus amplifying the targeted effect. By way of these steps, the product is no longer "natural." It now has a focused concentration typically for a single purpose; the purpose of dealing with an unwanted symptom. HOWEVER, now that it is in an altered or unnatural/ *man-made* state it is no longer completely metabolized by the body. That means it is not broken-down to usable components with the waste being harmlessly excreted from the human body. The result is the creating of toxic by-products that are often stored somewhere in the body and/or causing side-effects.

Herbs and spices are powerful aids to help the body help itself. Oft times they are equally as potent and effective as pharmaceutical medication. Herbs differ from drugs. They are in a natural state. Being natural, they produce fewer or no side-effects. This is because the by-products of herbs are easily metabolized, and the waste can be discarded by the body.

CAUTION: Pharmaceutical companies lose millions of dollars each year as more and more people seek health answers from vitamins and herbs rather than a pill or potion requiring a prescription and causing numerous side-effects. For this reason, big Pharma (the pharmaceutical industry) is lobbying heavily to make vitamins and herbs illegal without a prescription so they can produce them, control them and charge a great deal of money for them.

Ingesting vs. topical application

Eating, drinking and breathing are not the only ways to absorb toxins or nutrients for that matter. Remember, your skin is the largest organ of your body and it is highly absorptive. There are a number of topical medications, creams, lotions, make-up, sunscreens, bug repellants, etc., that are easy to apply by rubbing them on our skin. I would recommend you avoid putting anything on skin that you would not eat! Moisturizing lotion? Try coconut oil. Sunscreen? Find something made from natural products. I believe Dr. Mercola offers several items of this nature at his web site www.mercola.com

There remains a very important topic needing addressed in the *Toxins* portion of this book. It is one that is emotionally charged, causing an almost religious polarization between doctors, patients, friends and neighbors. The topic is vaccines.

Don't mistake me as some zealot, hell bent on non-vaccination and determined to convince parents everywhere to stop vaccinating their kids. Not in the least. But I am well-educated on the topic with a staggering amount of world research behind my educated decision to not vaccinate my children based on facts and findings. To not vaccinate or to "selectively vaccinate" is empowering and represents our God-given freedom of choice.

One, we should educate ourselves before making such a big decision since it can directly affect the health, longevity, and quality of life for ourselves, our children and grandchildren.

Two, we should never give up that right, yet it is slipping farther away every day.

How so?

Vaccines

Currently schools bully parents into believing their children are a health threat to other children if they are not fully vaccinated (Wrong! Research the facts). Often, principles will tell parents that their children cannot attend school without updating their vaccines. (Wrong again. We have the right to choose).

Certain states are in the process of passing legislation to make it literally "Against the Law" to not vaccinate yourself or your children, punishable by not only fines, but imprisonment. Wow, that sounds harsh for exercising your freedom to choose after hopefully making an educated decision. Does that sound like the America so many of us know and love?

Understand the facts.

Vaccination does not equal immunization

Let's start with proper definitions. "Vaccine" does not equal "Immunize," though the terms are used interchangeably in both medicine and media. There is a common commercial on TV and radio, "Immunize by 2, it's up to you." It is a brilliant marketing strategy training us to *believe* that we are purchasing or receiving the desired end result rather than the <u>chance</u> at the desired result.

According to Dorland's Medical Dictionary, a vaccine is "a suspension of attenuated or killed microorganisms...administered for prevention...or treatment of disease."

- The *vaccine* is the 'formula' that we inject into our children, our pets, our military personnel, etc.

- *Immunization* is the acquired resistance to a said microorganism obtained after our body and its innate intelligence has been exposed to that organism and has built up antibodies or an immune resistance to it. There are some microorganisms for which we simply have an inborn immunity. For example, a pet dog may become exposed to something that can make him very sick, but poses no health threat to humans. Likewise, we may be at risk of catching the flu each year due to a certain strain of virus, however, it poses no health threat to our dog.

When we weaken a virus or microorganism and inject it into our bloodstream to trigger an immunity building response, it is **no guarantee** that we will achieve the desired effect. Why? Because it is not a natural progression of how our incredibly complicated immune system works.

To share a simple example; the vaccine for chickenpox has been available for some time now. However, we are seeing vaccinated children who are getting the chickenpox, or experiencing shingles in their childhood or twenties.

What my wife and I chose to do was, in a controlled fashion, was simply expose our children to a natural form of the chickenpox. While living in Portugal, we heard that our friend's children had come down with the chickenpox. They would be stuck at home, unable to attend school for a couple of weeks. Great! We took our children over to play with their kids – a chicken pox "party". (**I do not recommend this for any other 'disease.'**) We then took care of our children at home for the next few weeks as their bodies adapted, overcame and developed *natural immunity* to the Vericella virus.

Statistics clearly show that natural immunity is vastly more effective and lasts longer than artificially injecting a vaccine and hoping for some sign of immunity. If any form of immunity is obtained by artificial means it is temporary in nature which justifies the push from pharmaceutical companies and pediatricians to promote **booster shots**.

It is surprising to me how a population will seemingly just follow along with the increasing number of vaccines being pushed upon us…with little to NO RESEARCH to back the effectiveness of the vaccines. There is NO RESEARCH to back the effectiveness of a booster shot. There is not a single drug company manufacturing vaccines that claims their vaccine can "cure" or guarantee the prevention of the targeted disease/ailment. According to Pediatrician Robert Mendelsohn, MD and a growing number of authors, "There is no convincing scientific evidence that mass inoculations can be credited with eliminating any childhood disease."

Wow! That is a serious statement, and it was made over 25 years ago. Yet look how vaccines continue to multiply in the "vaccine schedule."

Vaccine schedule

New vaccines are regularly being added to the schedule at an alarming rate.

1980	20 vaccines
2003	40 vaccines
2004	53 vaccines
2005	58 vaccines
2006	63 vaccines
2009	68 vaccines

36 of these vaccines are scheduled to be administered by 18 months of age. As fast as it is growing there is no sign of it stopping. Experimental vaccines can be added at any time. Would you believe an AIDS vaccine is in the works to be added to the schedule in the upcoming years? You couldn't pay me to inject HIV into my children or a perfect little new born grandbaby.

Why more and more vaccines? Not because we are faced with deadly diseases spreading like wildfire around the world, threatening to wipe out the human race. No, more are added because vaccines are a HUGE MONEY MAKER for pharmaceutical companies who profit on the fears of innocent parents and elderly who simply want to protect themselves and their children!

My children may have to choose between vaccines or jail time the way legislation is moving to take away our right to choose. Big Pharma is exercising its leverage to lobby for laws that force parents and military personnel to vaccinate or face fines and imprisonment.

The vaccine schedule doesn't stop with the kids. In 2009, with minimal media coverage the new ADULT vaccine schedule was introduced adding as many as **73 additional vaccines after the age of 18**.[35]

"No other country on earth has an adult schedule of vaccines. No other country on earth recommends 150 vaccines to its citizens." ~Tim O'Shea, Author of *The Sanctity of Human Blood: Vaccination I$ not Immunization.*

(NOTE: I encourage patients, friends and family, to educate themselves on the topic of vaccines. This is something too important to just follow the herd blindly. There are several good books on vaccines but if I had to recommend just one book, I would say, Tim O'Shea's book is a must read! I also have the book and audio book, "The Vaccine Conundrum." Available at www.drjayshetlin.com)

The new US adult schedule includes 45 flu shots by the age of 65! There may not be research on the effectiveness of vaccines or booster shots but there ARE many studies, case studies and empirical data showing some of the adverse effect of vaccines.

Flu shots still use Mercury and aluminum as preservatives so they have an almost endless shelf-life.

Hugh Fudenburg, MD a leading immunogeneticist in the year 2000 said,

"If an individual had 5 consecutive flu shots between 1970 and 1980, the chances of Alzheimer's Disease were 10 times greater than for those getting...no shots." [36]

That seems a huge risk to take for a very unlikely chance at immunity.

What most people do not understand about the flu virus, or any virus for that matter, is how they are constantly changing and mutating. For scientists to predict the "strain of virus" that will most likely be the culprit during the next flu season is nothing shy of impossible. Yet doctors try so they can prepare enough vaccine ahead of time.

Problem #1: Take a look at an English dictionary. THOUSANDS of words within the dictionary are made up from various combinations of 26 simple letters. Scientists are equivalently choosing "letters" from the "alphabet" and hoping one of the three "words" (vaccines) they come up with will be the correct strain of virus for next year's flu season.

Result: 10s of thousands of people across the country and around the world inject a virus directly into their blood stream, with heavy metals and other toxins used as preservatives, hoping for a positive result.

Result of that result:

- Healthy individuals notice little or no symptoms. or adverse effects, while their body tries to expel the toxins injected, directly bypassing many of its natural defenses.

- People with a weakened immune system just caused further damage by allowing the virus in the vaccine, or some other opportunistic microorganism from outside the body, to take hold resulting in illness.

Comments often heard by doctors include: "I got the shot this year and I didn't get the flu." Or "I got the shot and still got the flu this year." Truth of the matter, they both played Russian roulette with their immune system, and are one step closer to developing Alzheimer's.

A not-so-funny statistic to follow is wherever the flu vaccine is administered in mass inoculations; those are the populations where the most "flu-related" deaths occur year after year. Don't take my word for it; watch the news.

Let me get back to childhood vaccines for a moment.

"The greatest threat of childhood disease lies in the dangerous and ineffectual efforts made to prevent them through mass 'immunization'." –Robert Mendensohn, MD (Notice he even used 'immunization' incorrectly, it should be 'vaccination.')[37]

How dangerous are childhood diseases?

Most of the diseases we vaccinate kids for are self-limiting and not deadly. At least they are not in this modern day and age. As we have moved into an era of improved hygiene and indoor plumbing we have seriously reduced the spread and severity of many diseases.

According to the British Association for the Advancement of Science, childhood diseases decreased 90% between 1850 and 1940, paralleling improved sanitation and hygienic practices, well before 'mandatory' vaccination programs.

In Great Britain, the polio epidemic peaked in 1950, and had declined 82% by the time the vaccine was introduced there in 1956.

It looks like vaccines took all the glory for wiping out diseases that had already run their course through humanity.

Germ theory

The Germ Theory, at least the way we have been raised to think of it, has been a misconception from the beginning. Sure there are a few pathogens that are highly contagious but it is a very short list. Most spreadable ailments you and I face have a much more difficult challenge to get from one host to another. The human immune system is pretty amazing. It has many parts including the skin, saliva, tonsils, stomach acid, fighter white T-cells, Thymus, Lymph nodes, Spleen, and so on (all under the supervision and control of the nervous system, I might add).

If you are from a big family or have ever lived in a dorm and noticed someone becomes "sick" did that automatically translate into "everyone became sick?" No. Because the pathogen has to get past each person's individual immunity. Factors that affect our health and immunity are clearly discussed in this book including: proper sleep, positive attitude, minimizing stress, a healthy nervous system, proper nutrition and avoiding toxins to name a few. So, it might be common in a home of 6 that one or two others contract the same viral or bacterial infection but that is because their immune system was compromised. Pathogens are opportunists, they take hold in a body with a weak immune defense.

The mass media is a powerful tool to fuel the fears of parents. A couple of years ago it was the bird flu...we are all doomed! Scientists were working frantically to come up with a vaccine for mass inoculation. One US government official made over 5 million dollars in a few short months because he had financial ties to the company making the bird flu vaccine. Was it scandalous? Who really knows. Regardless, the world was scared and jumped at the opportunity to get another shot.

In 2009 there was the Swine Flu scare. Media hyped it up for a few weeks. Scientists were working on a vaccine. It was "spreading fast around the world" and was the next "Pandemic!" Its symptoms are like the regular flu but a new name means a new vaccine which means more $$ for some lucky pharmaceutical companies. "Pandemic?" Do the math. You had a much better chance of winning the lottery than dying from the Swine Flu.

How dangerous is Pertusis or Whooping cough?

- According to literature in a pediatric physician's office, "The chance of adverse reactions to the DPT vaccine were 1 in 1750 while the chances of dying from Pertussis each year were 1 in several million.[38]

- A medical study in the USA found that over 80% of children less than 5 years of age, who had contracted whooping cough, had been **fully vaccinated**.[39]

The Mumps and Chickenpox certainly are not deadly. Tetanus is incredibly rare, 50 cases per year in the entire USA.

The one that seems the most peculiar to me is Hepatitis B. Why do we give this to a perfect little newborn? This is a vaccine to "prevent" a disease that is transmitted either sexually or through IV drug use (dirty needles). If the parents are faithful to each other and they are not IV drug users, why should they be pressured into injecting Hepatitis B and (a list of other toxic vaccine constituents) directly into the blood stream of their precious little child? That just does not make sense.

What is in a Vaccine?

Aside from the dead or weakened virus / microorganism, vaccines may contain cells from various animal tissue used to weaken the target microorganism. All vaccines have components like: formaldehyde (embalming fluid), ethylene glycol (anti-freeze), aluminum, and mercury (thimerosal), just to name a few. [40]

I'm not making this stuff up.

We know that formaldehyde and ethylene glycol can cause cancer. Aluminum is a potent neurotoxin, which can cause much more neurologic mischief than just Alzheimer's disease. Mercury is the most toxic non-radioactive metal making it the third deadliest element on planet earth, just behind plutonium. It is easily stored in fatty brain tissue and is highly toxic to nerve cells causing permanent nerve damage.

Since 1997, we have heard how there is no research to connect vaccines (more specifically thimerosal) to Autism. Yet a simple comparison of mercury poisoning symptoms and those of Autism is a dead giveaway. Over the past four decades we have watched Autism explode from 1 in 10,000 kids to the current 1 in 68.The MMR and the use of Mercury in vaccines began at that time. Yet no one can connect the dots. Doctors try to blame genetics, yet most of these kids were perfectly normal healthy until after a series of vaccine where they regress to banging their heads on walls, lose the ability to communicate and develop digestive problems. Look at the work Jenny McCarthy and Jim Carrey have done with www.generationrescue.org, and tracking down solid research. The Autism rate was just 1/10,000 kids in 1983 when there were few vaccines compared to today. Now there are four times the childhood vaccines and 1/68 children with Autism. Generation Rescue recommend using the old vaccine schedule rather than the new one. [41]

In Utah statistics for Autism came in at 1/54[42] kids as of March, 2014. Is this higher because Utah parents are such good rule followers that they just line up and follow authority figures without asking questions? I don't know the answer; I just know it is a growing problem.

Congressman Dan Burton seems to have connected the dots. In 2002 he called a congressional hearing rebuking the National Institute of Health and the Center for Disease control for allowing vaccine manufacturers to produce their own "research" stating a vaccine is safe for public distribution. The NIH and the CDC just take the word of the manufacturers and require no further research. Tada! Stamp of approval and our kids become the real test market.

What Congressman Dan Burton also found was that in 100% of the cases where vaccines are approved and moved forward there are members on the "approval committee" that have direct financial ties to the product. The congressman's findings were scandalous. It is a system that lacks integrity. We have organizations established with names that sound like their purpose is to protect we, *the people*, like the "Food and Drug Administration" or the" National Institute of Health." Unfortunately, they do not function in that capacity.

The hearing aired on CSPAN, Congressman Burton showed footage of research that HE had funded (since no other organization was willing to actually perform research to prove or disprove the vaccine relation to Autism.) The independent research group presented astounding video footage of how even the smallest amount of mercury introduced near nerve tissue resulted in cell degeneration. In other words, a direct correlation between vaccines, thimerisol and Autism!

There are now doctors, scientists, and authors who have clearly linked these toxic injections to disease: from autism to auto immune disorders, even childhood cancer.

Did you catch that? In our overconfident effort to vaccinate and prevent non-life threatening diseases we are actually creating serious, life-long or life-threatening diseases.

This is a scary subject. Our natural response is denial. "No, that couldn't be. I don't want to believe that's happening." So we don't. We simply tune out the truth and follow the marketing propaganda.

I am not promoting this as some big "conspiracy theory" or the likes. However, we won't hear the truth on the news because of one very large factor: Business. It is all business. Big Pharma is the largest contributor of marketing campaigns in the media and one of the biggest, if not THE biggest, political supporter/lobbyist.

During the big flu pandemic of 1938, Truman passed a law stating that vaccine manufacturers could not be held liable for lawsuits regarding adverse reactions to any vaccines since the government was mandating them.

This opened a door for vaccines where manufacturers did not have to worry about negative financial repercussions due to lawsuits.

Adverse vaccine reactions were not tracked by physicians. Actually, they were not tracked by anyone. Why should they be? They were the miracle of the new era. Unfortunately, negative effects of vaccines followed and have continued to increase over the years. Cancer, a disease of the aged, became more prevalent in children. Asthma exploded and continues to increase, auto-immune disorders such as Lupus and Multiple Sclerosis are increasing. Unexplainable chronic conditions, such as fibromyalgia and chronic fatigue syndrome, Gulf War Syndrome have become much more common. Yet no one seems to make sense of the data.

As far as physician's responsibility for reporting adverse reactions, fathom this: mass vaccination programs have been rolling in the US since 1902. But until 1991, there was 'no central record keeping agency in the U.S. to which physicians could report vaccine reactions." The FDA estimates doctors only report about 10% of adverse reactions. A New York study found that 2%, at best, are reported.

In the 1980's President Reagan passed a law freeing drug companies of **any** responsibility should a child die from the side-effects of a vaccine.

A fund was established for families who had children hurt by vaccines. The fund was primarily paid by tax dollars and partially paid by drug companies. It is a difficult fund to access and few people know about it. Should a family be in the unfortunate circumstance to need help from that fund, they have to sue, and win their case, in order to receive a settlement. It costs thousands, even tens of thousands of dollars to do that. All settlements come with a "gag-order" meaning you will lose the money you won if you disclose how you got it, or if you help others (families with children injured by vaccines) know about the fund, system, or settlement.

Why was Congressman Dan Burton so emotionally charged at the hearing? His committee was working on a bill for homeland security. Just prior to it passing, someone slipped in a small addendum without his committee knowing (and it was passed). That addendum gave immunity to the government from any financial responsibility should anyone have adverse reactions to a vaccine.

Where does that leave us? Parents think they have to vaccinate because the media and the schools tell them it is "mandatory." It is NOT! And should their child have any negative 'effects' from the vaccine such as Autism they have absolutely nowhere to turn, no one to blame, and no place to get help. But they now have the life-long challenge of a "handicapped" child. A child that most likely will never fully function in society, likely will not marry, and is unlikely to become self-sufficient, thus permanently altering the parents' future, and the future of the child. The emotional and financial cost of disability caused by vaccination is incalculable.

To see Congressman Burton's footage, visit my website www.shetlin.com/media. (Call my office or send an e-mail to get the password since it is copyrighted material)

Parents cannot beat themselves up over something they didn't know. If you have a child with Autism or other adverse reactions to vaccines, look for answers. They are out there.

Freedom to choose

In conclusion regarding Toxins, avoid as many as possible. Get informed. Educate yourself regarding your rights regarding vaccination. Don't inject yourself or your children with harmful substances simply because you didn't know better. It is your responsibility to get informed.

Should you choose to vaccinate your children, do your homework first. Exercise your parental right to pick and choose what is given to your child and when. If you choose to vaccinate your children, my best advice is to **wait until they are over two years old** and follow the 1983 schedule.

Look at statistics from other countries, such as Japan, the Netherlands and several others; since they stopped vaccinating infants (in other words they have their citizens wait until the child is over two years old) their incidents of SIDs has dropped off the charts. I am still researching other side-effects.

Understand that infants **are not** miniature adults. "A single vaccine given to a 6-pound newborn is the same as giving a 180-lb adult 30 vaccines on the same day."[43]

Should you miss a schedule, don't play catch-up in a single doctor visit. Discuss with your physician or pediatrician options for spreading out the vaccines. Playing "catch-up" could cause a toxic overload on that helpless little body.

Be selective on the shots you really feel they should have. Don't be pressured into something your parental instincts are telling you your child does not need.

As mentioned earlier, sometimes the potential side-effects outweigh the disease being vaccinated against. Statistically, the chances of catching, or dying, from the particular disease is far less than the chance of negative side-effects.

Finally, you DO have choices. Most states still allow you to opt-out of vaccines and still allow kids in school for one of three reasons. You just need to sign an exemption form. If you live in Utah, Utah State Code 53A-11-302 allows an individual to be exempt from vaccinations if they do one of the following:

- A statement from a licensed physician stating that im-munization(s) could harm the child.

- A statement that the person has a personal belief against immunization.

- A statement that the person is a member of a religion whose teachings are against immunization.

Make your own affidavit of exemption.

1. On a piece of paper simply type the following:

Affidavit of Exemption

I hereby claim exemption to vaccinations because they may be harmful to my health or damaging to my immune system.

_____

Name

_____

Signature

_____

Date

---

2. Take it to a notary. Sign and date it. Make copies.

3. Send original to the entity requiring the shot. (a school, your work, etc)

4. Send a copy by certified mail to the Legal Department of the entity requiring the shots

5. Keep your copy.

To oppose your affidavit will now require more effort on their part so most will let it go.

Personally, I have never had any trouble with exemptions. I have had pressure from schools trying to motivate me to fully vaccinate my kids. Why do they do it?

- They don't know any better.

- Schools receive compensation from the State who receives compensation from drug companies.

For every fully vaccinated child, the state is granted $100 in federal funds. *~Orient, J, MD Statement of the Association of American Physicians & Surgeons to the Subcommittee on Government reform June 14, 1999*

Some schools are **allegedly** fined up to $2000 for every registered child who is not fully vaccinated *~A letter to me from Corral Cliffs Elementary school, St. George, UT - November 2003*

If this type of response is received, please ask for documentation. It is your right to full disclosure. Ask yourself what entity out there would fine a school because a parent chooses not to vaccinate? It simply does not exist.

I would like to give credit to the medical profession for its part in being proactive rather than reactive as far as the approach of vaccines. Vaccines are one of the few preventative approaches we see in medicine. Most modern medicine is involved in labeling a disease, then chasing the cure with a man-made treatment or drug. Where vaccines fail us is in their lack of research prior to mass distribution and the system being driven by pharmaceutical profits. This leads to more and more unnecessary vaccines full of toxic preservatives that accumulate in otherwise healthy human tissue, thereby causing a gamut of other diseases to plague humanity.

"Though society today views vaccines as cutting edge medicine, 100 years from now we will look back on vaccines the way you and I view leaching or bloodletting." *~Dr. Andrew Hatch, Portugal 2006*

TECHNIQUE FOR ADVANCED LIVING

Vaccines - Know your Options: It is impossible to get "immunized," you can only be "vaccinated." Vaccines are no guarantee of immunity. You have choices. Vaccinate when older. Limit vaccines only to the ones you feel are safe or you feel you need. YOU ARE THE BOSS OF YOUR BODY. People and organizations cannot force you to receive a vaccination shot. Guaranteed, any lawyer would be happy to take your case against them on charges of 'assault with a deadly weapon' due to the toxic nature of the preservatives used.

Before you are vaccinated or you vaccinate your children:

- Know the side-effects and the risks
- Weigh out which is worse, the disease vs. the potential side-effects and the statistical chances of each.
- Know your legal options should you vaccinate. Who is responsible if you have an adverse reaction?
- Follow your heart.

Toxins vs. nutrients in our daily meals

As stated at the beginning of this chapter, some "sources of nutrition" can actually be loaded with toxins.

How we choose to shop can make a big difference in the number of toxins we ingest with our nutrients. For example, in our metropolitan lifestyle, convenience is king. Meals from a can or a box are popular and easy to prepare. Microwaves provide fast heat but kill or denature many nutrients. It is all about speed in the USA because eating is almost an inconvenience. That is why we are the "Fast-food" nation. In some countries, EATING is still almost a sacred pastime. Portugal was a real eye-opener for me and my family. In 2005, there was only one drive-through restaurant in the entire country. The Portuguese view dining as quality time spent visiting with family, friends, or co-workers. It is not rushed, but rather cherished. The result is people actually enjoy their food, digest it properly, and build quality relationships with the friends and family over a meal. It took me nearly two months living in Portugal to finally adapt and enjoy my meals rather than push through them to get on with the 'event' that followed eating, be it work, a movie, etc. My American mentality was to eat fast and go! Soon I noticed that at every restaurant we went to, the meal was hand-prepared. Products were fresh and often purchased at the same store or farmer's market where I shopped. Typical fruits and vegetables bought at the local store were what we Americans would label 'organic,' without having to pay triple the cost, or having to find them in a special section. Meat and poultry were also what we would consider 'organic.' The first month there I walked past a restaurant that I thought was a cat rotisserie. The meat in the window was scrawny and looked strange to me. I soon discovered, and to my 'taste buds' delight, it was a rotisserie chicken shop. Unlike in mainstream America the chickens were raised without all the steroids and antibiotics that artificially inflated the size of the chickens and their breasts.

I soon learned that NO American beef is imported into Europe because the quality and conditions of our beef is substandard to the legal requirements of the European Union.

So what do we do in the States to minimize toxic overload from the many different food sources we have and use each day? Shop strategically.

All grocery stores have a similar layout. For the most part, stick to the periphery of the store. The center usually contains all the processed and frozen goods. The outer isles are baked goods, <u>fresh fruits</u>, <u>fresh vegetables</u>, <u>meat</u> and <u>dairy</u>.

Still, fresh fruits and vegetables are often covered in chemical bug repellants. These are deadly to bugs, and certainly unhealthy to humans. So, unless you spend a lot of money for organic or raise them yourself, be sure to wash your fruit and veggies very well. I have heard some controversial arguments that say even organic fruits and vegetables may have chemical 'spill over' since organic fields and regular fields are often adjacent to each other. Living in Korea, I noticed, a similar problem with heavy pesticides. Consequently, Koreans peel all their fruits. Some authors are extreme enough to say only eat organic or only eat XYZ brands of fruits or vegetables. I want to help you avoid toxins and increase your nutrient intake with what is readily available. I recommend you buy local fruits and vegetables, and then wash them thoroughly. Whenever possible, grow your own. Have your own private garden. Canning your own fruits and vegetables is both healthy and rewarding.

As far as toxins in processed foods, there are many chemicals, and so little real food in the container. Make it a habit to read the labels. Many of your canned foods, even vegetables, have high fructose corn syrup as one of the primary ingredients. This is a concentrated sugar that is cheap for manufacturers to make.

TOXINS

Footnotes:

34. Wikipedia.org "Toxin"

35. 2009 Child, Adolescent and Adult Immunization Schedule www.cdc.gov The Sanctity of Human Blood 13th Edition; Tim O'Shea

    2016 same

36. Fudenberg, H MD Hazards of Vaccines Journal of Clinical investigation. Vol. 3 p97-105, 2000 quoted in The Sanctity of Human Blood 13th edition

37. How to Raise a Healthy Child...In Spite of Your Doctor; 1984 Pediatrician Robert S. mendelsohn, MD

38. Alan Phillips, independent investigator quoting a vaccine pamphlet found in a pediatrician's office

39. New England Journal of Medicine. July 1994

40. Physician's Desk Reference 2007

41. Are we poisoning our kids in the name of protecting their health?, www.generationrescue.org

42. In Utah statistics for Autism came in at 1 in 54 according to UtahAutismRegistry.org

43. Haley, B PhD http://wale.to/v/hale.html via The Sanctity of Human Blood

    Also his video testimony on CSPAN when testifying to Senator Dan Burton - available on Shetlin.com

11. Haley

NUTRITION

Our body needs certain "building blocks" called nutrients in order to sustain life. Organic nutrients include carbohydrates, fats, proteins or amino acids, and vitamins. Inorganic nutrients include natural resources and minerals. There are many things we can eat to sustain life that are not necessarily "nutritious" or good for us; thus the term, "malnutrition," or as I call it, "bad building blocks."

Nutrition is fundamentally important and is grossly misunderstood by the general public. It is important for every adult or parent to understand some basics in this area for their own health and, additionally, for the health of their children. As a nation, or a world for that matter, it is critical we strive to be more health conscious with children in order to curb the exploding trend of obesity and diseases such as diabetes, asthma, and others that are on the rise with roots in our nutrition and lifestyle habits.

We are all victims of marketing gurus who know how to visually push our appetite buttons. Junk food, snacks and drinks with poor nutritional value are constantly being marketed to us. They are conveniently placed in the grocery store and are *often cheaper to purchase than healthier items*. According to some authors, many of the chemicals and ingredients on snack labels (the ingredients you can't pronounce), are *addictive in nature*. This keeps us going back for more. Thus once they have us hooked, it is easier, thus cheaper, to keep us coming back again and again. This allows for a lower price point to make it easy for us to stay stuck in that cycle. Sadly, we form unhealthy eating habits. This robs our body of the necessary building blocks required to stay strong and vibrant. Instead we are stuck in a rut of empty calories and man-made chemicals. [Read the labels on a bag of chips]. Unfortunately, these foods rob us of the energy and the drive to be active.

Supplements

There are literally thousands of nutritional supplements on the market today. It seems new ones are being added regularly. Lately, each new one tries to come up with a "one-hit-wonder" usually a drink that will give your body "everything it needs." "Super food," is another title being thrown around. There are several nutritional beverages both at the grocery store and sold in an MLM format. We have a great deal to choose from.

Bottom line, most of us need supplemental nutrients. I recommend something liquid-based; however, I have yet to see a single product that meets all the nutritional needs of an individual. Powdered greens are a great place to start. They provide an affordable way to get 8 to 15 servings of fruits and vegetable in a liquid form. Medical text books suggest we absorb 98% of the nutrients in liquid form vs. only 12-15% once something is in a pill.

Cells have memory

The body has memory, even on a cellular level. Individuals who are more active when they are younger have an easier time trimming down or toning up as compared to someone who may have been sedentary at a young age. Consider the following: a weight lifter who stops lifting for a couple of years tones up quicker, once he starts working out again, than someone who has never lifted weights. Why? Because muscle cells have memory.

On a similar but more disturbing note, there is arguable evidence that children under the age of 12 are actually growing or increasing the NUMBER of fat cells in their body composition based on what they eat, how much exercise they get and how overweight they are. Adults, on the other hand, are simply filling and emptying their set number of fat cells. Therefore, a child who is overweight under the age of 12 will have numerically more fat cells in adolescence and their adult years than they would if they had maintained a leaner body mass in their childhood. This may very well cause an increased difficulty to maintain a healthy weight when older. Not impossible, just more difficult.

This theory makes sense. However, I believe it could affect an individual beyond the age of 12. I suspect this is applicable up to finishing high school. We are still developing and growing until roughly the age of 23. I have seen several kids who struggle with weight challenges in high school and continued after. Even the boys trying out for football in high school are loading up with calories to put on weight and hopefully muscle mass as well. Many of these individuals find controlling their weight quite challenging after high school because they have reduced the intensity level of their activities.

I am not saying this is a hard-and-fast rule. In fact, anything is possible. Anyone who educates themselves on how to get better nutrition in their body and reduces toxins is heading in the right direction. Apply that education with exercise and discipline (remember the passion)…Voilá! An individual can more successfully control their weight.

This formula isn't rocket science. It's elementary algebra: x + y = z

- Caloric Intake +/- metabolism = your fitness number
- Eating right + Exercise = Better Health
- **Eat junk** + Exercise ≠ Better Health
- Eating Right + **No exercise** ≠ Better Health

Cardio burns calories and strengthens the cardiovascular system. Weight training or resistance exercises increase muscle mass which increases metabolism and burns calories. BOTH ARE IMPORTANT. Muscle weighs more than fat so do not base your health improvements directly on your weight. Rather, base it on how you feel, how the shape of your body is changing, and how your clothes fit.

Balanced nutrition is important because excess sugar is quickly and easily turned to fat or energy storage for later use. This is why, as a nation, we need to stop giving kids candy at every opportunity. It is almost an American dietary staple. There are pop machines and candy machines in most schools. It seems like every time you go to the bank, or other offices they have suckers or some kind of candy for the children of visiting customers. The list goes on. Kids simply have too much access to sweets these days.

The easiest way to lose weight (unwanted fat) is an "imbalanced diet." This is a means to an end because an imbalanced diet; 1) should be practiced under medical supervision, 2) involves ketosis or a metabolic state that increases fat burn while preserving muscle mass and 3) requires no exercise. In fact, it is counterproductive to exercise while in ketosis. For these reasons it is not something to continue for a lifetime. I won't go into the details of a ketosis diet in this book but you can research on you own diet programs such as "Ideal Protein." Very effective but it is a short term solution for those with a large amount of weight to lose. Keytosis diets require minimal consumption of carbs or sugars. Once a goal weight is reached, the "exit strategy" still required a solid "balanced diet" with a lifestyle change that includes exercise. Let's talk about sugars.

Sugars

Sugars are an important part of our diet but they should be the right kinds in the right quantities. Excess of the wrong sugars not only promote tooth decay, but obesity, diabetes, and a suppressed immune system.

Good Sweeteners...

Fructose: Sugar from fruits and vegetables is called 'fructose.' It is the simplest form of sugar. It is easily absorbed and used for energy. You can even buy fructose in crystal form at the health food store to use in cooking. It comes from dried fruits and looks just like sucrose or table sugar. It is, however, sweeter and requires one/half to one/third less the amount to supply the same sweetness to your recipes. It is also less toxic to your body. That does not mean eat it by the spoonful, simply it is a better sweetener for our body. I still recommend moderation with any sweetener.

Honey: Honey, of course, is a great natural sweetener. Honey from your local area, produced by your local bees and local plant pollen, can actually be quite helpful to your body with local plant allergies as well.

Raw/Unrefined Brown Sugar: This is simply sucrose sugar that is brown in color because of the molasses that remains with the sucrose crystals. Molasses does contain calcium and iron where sucrose has no nutritional value, only calories. So brown sugar is slightly better than table sugar, but not by much.

Molasses: Molasses, the concentrated liquid extract of the sugar-refining process, has been used since 325 B.C. in baking and confectionery products. Molasses can be extracted from cane or beets, but foods primarily use sugar-cane-derived molasses.

Fancy Molasses is an excellent source of iron, calcium, and vitamin

B and serves as a great energy food.

Fancy Molasses - also known as Gold Star, when used in baking, the results are a light colored, sweet product, also good as a topping on bread, biscuits, and crackers.

Lite Molasses - contains 40% less sugar than Fancy Molasses. Recipes made with Light Molasses have a subtle flavor, and are lighter in color. Cookies are slightly softer while breads are crustier. Light molasses comes from the first boiling of the sugar.

Cooking Molasses - is a blend of Fancy and Blackstrap Molasses. The use of Cooking Molasses results in a darker, less sweet baked product (great for ginger snaps).

Unsulphured Molasses - has the best flavor, is made from sun-ripened cane which has grown 12-15 months.[44]

Pure Maple Syrup: Maple syrup contains about 67% solids of which about 89% is sucrose; the remainder is primarily fructose and glucose, with traces of other sugars. Maple syrup is produced by heat, or increasingly with reverse osmosis to remove about 90% of the water, with no added ingredients, and must reach 66° Bx (degrees brix) in order to legally be "pure maple syrup". It possesses some nutritional value, containing calcium (greater than milk, by volume), potassium (more than bananas, by weight), manganese, magnesium, phosphorous, iron, and thiamin. It also contains traces of vitamins B2, B5, B6, B7 and B9, and many amino acids and phenolic compounds. A serving that includes 50 ml of maple syrup contains the following recommended daily allowances: Calcium 6%, Iron 5%, Manganese 2%, Thiamin 6%, Riboflavin 2%. Its caloric value is around 40 per tablespoon (15 ml), compared with 64 for honey and 60 for corn syrup.[45]

Bad Sweeteners...

Sucrose: The most common form of sugar. It is bleached sugar or table sugar.

Sacrin/splenda/equal: Man-made chemical artificial sweeteners. These are commonly used by diabetics for sweeteners. I would strongly advise avoiding these. Once you are a diabetic, your choices are limited. Some of these display the properties of a neuro-toxin, meaning they negatively affect our nervous system. More importantly, the purpose of an artificial sweetener for diabetics (people who no longer readily produce insulin in the pancreas) is to offer sweetness without raising the blood sugar levels which would require more insulin in the blood to uptake the sugar. However, the body is still fooled into thinking the blood sugar levels are up, so the next thing eaten may very easily be turned to storage or fat. A common quick snack in the USA is a diet drink, for the reduced calories, along with a candy bar, to hold off hunger until the next meal. This is the "perfect combination" to pack on unwanted pounds!

High Fructose Corn Syrup: This is a great product for manufacturers, awful for consumers. It is cheap to make and a potent sweetener. IT IS IN ALMOST EVERY PROCESSED FOOD TODAY. Thus, if we are eating or drinking even a few processed foods each day we are taking into our bodies far more refined sugar than we realize. Look on the next can of beans you buy. Read the label of any soft drink or popular energy drink today. Notice it is not just ON the label, but it's in the top two or three ingredients. Ingredients are listed in order of quantity from most to least. Meaning, most of what you are eating or drinking is sugar! Too much of anything can be TOXIC. Any of the sugars listed above are no different.

Agava: According to Michael Wayne PhD. and Dr. Joseph Mercola, Agava is actually worse than High Fructose Corn Syrup. Yes, it is a sweetener that comes from Blue Agava which when fermented makes Taquila but it is made primarily of fructose and glucose in very high concentrations.

Concentrations are so high that it can trigger "metabolic syndrome," a topic we discuss at length in the office during our nutrition and weight loss classes.

Agava may be a "natural type" of sweetener, as it comes from a plant but it certainly is not good for you and is advised to use in very small portions or not at all.

Reading Labels

The labels show nutritional value, and a list of ingredients. The list displays the ingredients from the most to the least. If you are a pop drinker you will see something like…

INGREDIENTS: CARBONATED WATER, HIGH FRUCTOSE CORN SYRUP, CARAMEL COLORS, NATURAL AND ARTIFICIAL FLAVORS, POTASSIUM (PRESERVATIVE)	Guess what it is.

As you can see a can of soda is made of mostly water and cheap sugar. Most sodas have about 10 teaspoons of sugar per serving. Guess the following soda.

INGREDIENTS: CARBONATED WATER, HIGH FRUCTOSE CORN SYRUP, NATURAL FLAVORS, CITRIC ACID, SODIUM BENZIATE (PRESERVATIVE FRESHNESS), CAFFEINE, SODIUM CITRA`E, GUM ARABIC, CALCIUM DISODIUM EDTA (TO PROTECT FLAVORS), BROMINATED VEGETABLE OIL, PANAX GINSENG ROOT EXTRACT, BLUE1, RED 40

This small bottle contains 290 calories, of course, all from sugar. Running for 20 to 30 minutes at your target heart rate could burn off that many calories. The problem with soda is most people have several per day or the infamous "Big Gulp" which is the sugar calorie equivalent of an extra meal, some 1200 to 1500 calories all from sugar.

[The first example was Root beer and the second was Mountain Dew]

Suggestion, learn to love water. Water with your meals will save you literally hundreds of dollars each year and literally thousands of low quality calories.

A few label examples from canned fruits and vegetables:

GREEN BEANS	KIDNEY BEANS	PEARS
INGREDIENTS: GREEN BEANS, WATER, SALT	INGREDIENTS: DARK KIDNEY BEANS, WATER, SUGAR, SALT, CALCIUM CLORIDE (to help maintain firmness) DISODIUM EDTA (to help promote color retention)	INGREDIENTS: PEARS, WATER, CORN SYRUP, SUGAR
Not bad		*Not great*

Take the time to read the labels. Check for sugars being close to the beginning of the ingredient list. Look where the calories are coming from and how many per serving. And watch for words you don't know or can't even pronounce.

Canned fruits and vegetables are fantastic for food storage. Nutritionally speaking, fresh is best, frozen is second, and canned is third. Remember, flash-frozen fruits and vegetables retain 10 times the amount of nutrients as canned fruits and vegetables.

WHAT DOES REFINED SUGAR REALLY DO TO THE BODY?

An excellent chart on pp 68-72 of Appleton's book gives a quick overview. Some excerpts:

Refined sugar:

- Suppresses the immune system
- Makes the blood acidic
- Advances aging
- Decreased blood flow to the heart
- Increases liver and kidney size

and refined sugar causes:

- Mineral deficiencies, especially chromium, copper, calcium and magnesium
- Tooth decay
- Digestive disorders
- Arthritis
- Asthma
- Candida albicans
- Hyperactivity in children
- Osteoporosis
- Kidney damage
- Food allergies
- Eczema
- Atherosclerosis

- Free radical formation
- Loss of enzyme
- Function
- Brittle tendons
- Migraines
- Blood clots
- Depression

Footnotes:

44. *Sweet Deception,* Dr. Joseph Mercola 2006

45. *Sweet Deception,* Dr. Joseph Mercola 2006

SWEET POISON

THE DANGERS OF ARTIFICIAL SWEETENERS

What is the real difference between TRUE sweeteners and ARTIFICIAL sweeteners? To answer that we will have to take a look at molecular structure, which means we'll be talking about organic chemistry. Don't worry; it will be easier than you think.

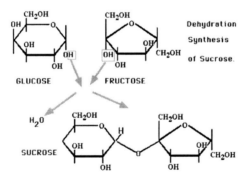

Let's start from the beginning. Most people have a "sweet tooth" or at least appreciate the delicious and almost addictive nature of the palatable sweetness sugar delivers. Before chocolates and candies, the delightful and refreshing taste of fruit was used for desserts. FRUCTOSE or the simple sugar molecule found in most fruits is deliciously sweet and easy for the body to digest.

Through the years the human race, especially Americans, have developed a growing 'casual addiction' to sweets. Molasses was used as a sweetener in early manufactured products. Through the years sugar cane and white processed sugar became less expensive to generate in large quantities, and easier to use in countless products from cola beverages to canned goods. Today it is difficult to buy any processed, canned or bottled food or beverage without sugar additives. High Fructose Corn Syrup (HFCS) is an inexpensive and popular sweetener today. You even find it in canned vegetables.

100 years ago the average American ate less than 5 lbs of sugar per year...today that average is over 158 lbs per year. That's for a single person! Wow, what a big change!

Sucralose

With the increase of sugar intake in our society, certain side-effects have become noticeable in the general population: dental cavities, obesity (with its subsequent health complications), hyperactivity, and Type II diabetes, to name a few.

It is not human nature to revert to the habits of the past when doing so is perceived as self-denial. However, something needed to be done by the food industry to help curb this overwhelming increase of sugar consumption. The answer: artificial sweeteners.

These sugar alternatives are usually hundreds or thousands of times sweeter than natural sugars, thus requiring less quantity and fewer calories per serving of sweet flavor. In the 70's, as people became more calorie conscious, and with the rise of diabetes, artificial sweeteners or "sugar substitutes" had a marketing edge.

The food industry began using artificial sweeteners in more and more products, some from "natural sources" and others being man-made. Some of the popular ones were discovered in laboratories, strictly "by accident."

Sweet Poisons

In 1879 at John Hopkins University, two researchers were working with toluene derivatives and other toxic chemicals used in making gasoline, paint thinners, fingernail polish and the likes. One of the scientists spilled the toluene derivative onto his hand and later noticed his food at dinner tasted oddly sweet. He traced the taste back to the chemicals and named the substance saccharine after the word saccharide, which means, complex sugar. [Surprisingly, saccharin may be the safest artificial sweetener on the market. However, there is correlation between saccharin and cancer, particularly bladder cancer. Hmm…what we don't know CAN hurt us.]

Saccharin

Aspartame was discovered in 1965. It dominated the artificial sweetener market until Splenda came along in the late nineties. Aspartame goes by several other names including NutraSweet® and Equal®. "Today it is sold in over one hundred countries, found in over six thousand products, and is consumed by over 250 million people. It's found in most diet sodas and a good portion of chewing gum." It too was discovered by accident in a lab. A scientist, working on a drug to treat peptic ulcer disease, licked his finger to pick up a piece of paper and got the first taste of aspartame.

Interestingly, 10% of the molecule is methanol aka "wood alcohol." The majority of the molecule is made up of two amino acids.

When these two amino acids are found in normal food with other amino acids there is no problem. When they are alone and in high concentration, they seep into the nervous system acting as toxic nerve agents. They create excessive firing of brain neurons. This is called *excitotoxicity* by Dr. Russell Blaylock. This can cause headaches, mental confusion, depression, balance problems and seizures.[46] It functions as one of the best ant poisons. How? It is a neurotoxin so it most likely kills the ants by interfering with their nervous system. [Other research has shown links to brain tumors, lymphatic cancer,[47] irreversible genetic damage, fatigue, chest tightness, sleeping problems, burning skin, fertility problems, low birth weight and memory problems such as Alzheimer's symptoms. Personally, I suspect it is a contributing factor to Gulf-War Syndrome from cans of diet drinks sitting in the sun prior to consumption by troops.]

Splenda is one of the greatest public dupes in history. Marketing spins such as "made from real sugar," lead the public to believe it is safe and natural. Splenda is the brand name for sucralose. Even the name sucralose is misleading (on purpose) to look similar to sucrose which is table sugar. However, sucralose is a chlorinated artificial sugar. It's proper name is, "1/6-dichloro1,6dideoxy-beta-D-fructofuranosyl-4-chloro-4-deoxy-alpha-D-galactopyranoside."

Chloride vs. Chlorine

The fact that there are 'little green attachments' on the sucralose molecule image shown below should be troubling to any reader. These represent chlorine.

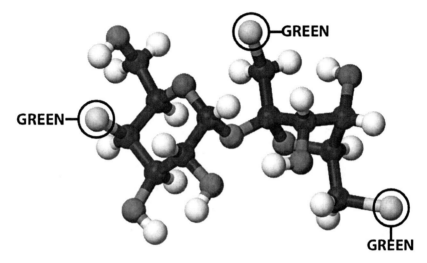

Chlorine gas is one of the most toxic chemicals known to man and is not found in nature. It was used as a poisonous gas in WWI, killing almost 100,000 soldiers and hospitalizing over 1 million.[48]

Without getting overly scientific, to manufacture Splenda, hydrogen atoms are artificially replaced with chlorine. These bonds are unstable (unlike NaCl or table salt which is found in nature and is quite stable). The unstable chlorine bonds of sucralose can deliver toxic chlorine directly into our cells.[49] [Some of the side-effects proven and still in question include: damaging cellular DNA, fertility issues, cancer, decreased urination, enlarged colon, enlarged liver and brain; shrunken ovaries, enlarged and calcified kidneys, increased adrenal cortical hemorrhaging, abnormal liver cells, growth retardation, and damage to the immune system.]

Why are people willing to subject their bodies to these chemicals? Two simple reasons:

1. Marketing has done an impressive job leading the public to think that artificial sweeteners are "good for you." The public now thinks these substitutes are great for people with diabetes, and that the low calorie count will help everyone else lose weight.

2. The public does not understand the true risks behind the pseudo rewards.

Research by the University of Texas Health Science Center at San Antonio showed that, rather than promoting weight loss, the use of diet drinks was a marker for increasing weight gain and obesity. Those that consumed diet soda were more likely to gain weight than those that consumed naturally-sweetened soda.[50]

My thoughts on artificial sweeteners and weight gain have long been in agreement with UTHSCSA research findings. *I suspect that beverages with artificial sweeteners may have fewer calories in them but the artificial sweetener molecules still fool the body into thinking that blood sugar levels are elevated. For a **non**-diabetic the body will then release insulin. Since we rarely have a diet drink by itself, the next thing we eat goes straight to storage or fat. I don't know how many times I have seen an obese person with a diet drink and a Snickers bar or a diet drink and a value meal. That Snickers bar or that value meal gets processed straight to fat storage…the exact opposite of what the individual is trying to accomplish by 'reducing their calorie intake' with a diet beverage.*

What I have recently learned may surprise you. Labeling laws allow the use of "sugar-free" if the serving size is less than 0.5 grams of sugar, and "calorie-free" if the serving size is less than 5 calories. Thus, **most artificial sweetener packets are at least 96 percent sugar!** Even worse, Splenda® No Calorie Sweetener is 99 percent sugar and only 1 percent sucralose."[51]

Diabetics beware! Artificial sweeteners are not all they are cracked up to be.

Stevia. "If you've ever tasted stevia, you know it's extremely sweet. In fact, this non-caloric herb, native to Paraguay, has been used as a sweetener and flavor enhancer for centuries. But this innocuous-looking plant has also been a focal point of intrigue in the United States in recent years because of actions by the U.S. Food and Drug Administration.

The subject of searches and seizures, trade complaints and embargoes on importation, stevia has been handled at times by the FDA as if it were an illegal drug.

Since the passage of the Dietary Supplement Health and Education Act (DSHEA), stevia can be sold legally in the United States, but only as a "dietary supplement." Even so, it can be found in many forms in most health-food stores and is becoming more regularly available at regular grocery stores. It is also incorporated into drinks, teas and other items (all labeled as "dietary supplements"). Currently, it cannot, however, be called a "sweetener" or even referred to as "sweet." To do so would render the product "adulterated," according to the FDA, and make it again subject to seizure."[52]

"According to Dr. Zoltan Rona, MD - a source who Martini quotes in her article - there has never been a reported case of any adverse reaction to stevia." To date, this seems to be the safest alternative, especially for diabetics. Time will tell.

The following table is copied directly from wikipedia:

"The three primary compounds used as sugar substitutes in the United States are saccharin (e.g., Sweet'N Low), aspartame (e.g., Equal, NutraSweet) and sucralose (e.g., Splenda). In many other countries cyclamate and the herbal sweetener stevia are used extensively.

The following table is copied directly from wikipedia:

"The three primary compounds used as sugar substitutes in the United States are saccharin (e.g., Sweet'N Low), aspartame (e.g., Equal, NutraSweet) and sucralose (e.g., Splenda). In many other countries cyclamate and the herbal sweetener stevia are used extensively.

Natural sugar substitutes

Brazzein	Protein, 800× sweetness of sucrose (by weight)
Curculin	Protein, 550× sweetness (by weight)
Erythritol	0.7× sweetness (by weight), 14× sweetness of sucrose (by food energy), 0.05× energy density of sucrose
Fructose	1.7× sweetness (by weight and food energy), 1.0× energy density of sucrose
Glycyrrhizin	50× sweetness (by weight)
Glycerol	0.6× sweetness (by weight), 0.55× sweetness (by food energy), 1.075× energy density, E422
Hydrogenated starch hydrolysates	0.4×–0.9× sweetness (by weight), 0.5×–1.2× sweetness (by food energy), 0.75× energy density
Lactitol	0.4× sweetness (by weight), 0.8× sweetness (by food energy), 0.5× energy density, E966
Lo Han Guo	300× sweetness (by weight)
Mabinlin	Protein, 100× sweetness (by weight)
Maltitol	0.9× sweetness (by weight), 1.7× sweetness (by food energy), 0.525× energy density, E965

Maltooligosaccharide Mannitol

0.5× sweetness (by weight), 1.2× sweetness (by food energy), 0.4× energy density, E421

Miraculin   Protein, does not taste sweet by itself, but modifies taste receptors to make sour things taste sweet temporarily

Monellin   Protein, 3,000× sweetness (by weight)

Pentadin   Protein, 500× sweetness (by weight)

Sorbitol   0.6× sweetness (by weight), 0.9× sweetness (by food energy), 0.65× energy density, E420

Stevia   250× sweetness (by weight)

Tagatose   0.92× sweetness (by weight), 2.4× sweetness (by food energy), 0.38× energy density

Thaumatin   Protein, 2,000× sweetness (by weight), E957

Xylitol   1.0× sweetness (by weight), 1.7× sweetness (by food energy), 0.6× energy density, E967

Artificial sugar substitutes

Note that because many of these have little or no food energy, comparison of sweetness based on energy content is not meaningful.

Acesulfame   potassium

200× sweetness (by weight), Nutrinova, E950, FDA Approved 1988

Alitame   2,000× sweetness (by weight), Pfizer, Pending FDA Approval

Aspartame   160–200× sweetness (by weight), NutraSweet, E951, FDA Approved 1981

117

Salt of aspartame-acesulfame
350× sweetness (by weight), Twinsweet, E962

Cyclamate   30× sweetness (by weight), Abbott, E952, FDA Banned 1969, pending re-approval

Dulcin   250× sweetness (by weight), FDA Banned 1950

Glucin   300× sweetness (by weight)

Neohesperidin dihydrochalcone
1,500× sweetness (by weight), E959

Neotame   8,000× sweetness (by weight), NutraSweet, FDA Approved 2002

P-4000   4,000× sweetness (by weight), FDA Banned 1950

Saccharin   300× sweetness (by weight), E954, FDA Approved 1958

Sucralose   600× sweetness (by weight), Splenda, Tate & Lyle, E955, FDA Approved 1998

Isomalt   0.45×–0.65× sweetness (by weight), 0.9×–1.3× sweetness (by food energy), 0.5× energy density, E953"

TECHNIQUE FOR ADVANCED LIVING

Sweet tooth

- Monitor your sugar intake
- Utilize healthy sugars, and start avoiding bad ones
- If you lower your sugar intake and reduce your "sweet" snacks, your desire for sweets will soon decrease

Artificial Sweeteners:

- Rule of thumb - Just say, "No!"
- Diet drinks – Just say, "No!"
- Drink more WATER – It is better for you and usually FREE.

Footnotes:

46. Russell Blaylock, Excitotoxins: The Taste that Kills. MD Health Press (NM) 1996

47. *Sweet Deception*, Dr. Joseph Mercola 2006

48. http://www.spartacus.schoolnet.co.uk/FWWgas.htm

49. Mercola & H.C. Grice and L.A. Goldsmith, "Sucralose an Overview of the Toxicity Date," Food and Chemical Toxicology 38 (2000): S1-S6

50. https://www.healthyhorns.utexas.edu/n_dietsoda.html

51. *Sweet Deception*, Dr. Joseph Mercola 2006

52. *Sweet Deception*, Dr. Joseph Mercola 2006

HARRISON • PART III

Little by little, Harrison made good improvements. But he was still far behind "the curve." At 9 months most kids are crawling, some are even walking; Harrison could roll around like crazy, but he could not sit up on his own. He was still quite 'floppy.' A child being able to crawl is incredibly important, not only for motor skill development, but for proper brain function. At times I would worry — almost panic — that he just wasn't making improvements fast enough. Then I would remember the impression I had to do what I knew he needed, and be patient. It seems the week after one of my 'worry spells' he would break through to the next level. So I stuck with the plan.

We kept his nerves flowing properly with Chiropractic adjustments, filled him with good nutrients and kept the toxins out. Today, I would call that regiment "Techniques for Advanced Living" — *laying down the "blue prints," putting the right nutritional "building blocks" in place, and avoiding toxins.*

It took Harrison till he was about a year and a half old before he finally started crawling. Whew! I have to admit I let out a huge sigh of relief at that milestone.

About that time, we experienced a series of challenges caused me to move my practice and family from the small town of St. George to the metropolis of Salt Lake City, Utah. In the interim of making the move, Shannon and I went to Europe for an International Chiropractic Convention. The convention was held in Athens, Greece. While there we met a gem of a human being, Dr. Andrew Hatch who practices Chiropractic in Portugal. He was at the seminar in search of good doctors to move to Portugal as associate physicians and help him open more clinics. He showed us footage of his office, the layout, style, and the software used. I was impressed by the similarities to my own practice, and yet, the differences that took it to an extraordinary new level of practice. On the plane home I had the strongest impression that Portugal was where we needed to be for the next few years. (Shannon and I had discussed several times in the past about the challenges of moving to Europe. She expressed to me a fair argument that she had spent her entire life learning to read lips in English. Why would she want to move to a foreign land with a foreign tongue?) Well, my heart of hearts was telling me that Portugal was where we needed to be. To my surprise, Shannon agreed.

Shortly after returning to the US, everything fell into place facilitating the move. We sold everything at garage sale prices, the six of us put our remaining belongings into our 15 checkable and carry-on bags, and our family moved halfway around the world.

The cobblestone sidewalks, cement walls, tile stairs and floors of Portugal were not easy on little Harrison. At the age of two he slowly learned to walk, and, like other children, he took many tumbles. Unfortunately, his coordination was reduced, so he simply could not catch himself like other kids. It was as if his reflexes couldn't get his little arms out fast enough to break his fall or protect his head and face. He had a lot of hard landings with no carpet or padding to soften the impact.

We soon invested in a little yellow bike helmet to protect his head. The cobblestone sidewalks were challenging even to adults as I witnessed many grown-ups face-plant on the streets of Portugal due to lose cobblestones. They presented an "obstacle course" to Harrison.

We persisted with our Advanced Living plan: blueprints (nerve flow), building blocks (good nutrients), and avoiding toxins. This seemed much easier living in Europe because their eating habits and lifestyle are clearly different. We were able to help Harrison (and ourselves) by eating more fish, olive oil, home cooked meals, and organic fruits and vegetables. Just walking on the sidewalks and the beaches seemed to be the physical therapy he needed. Blueprints, building blocks, avoiding toxins…

Harrison — Age 2

123

FAT OR FICTION

Fats

The difference between Fats and Oils: Simply put, fats are solid at room temperature while oils are not.

The civilized world, through the power of marketing, has developed a "fat phobia." This has, unfortunately, been a leading contributor to an American epidemic that has now grown to a world epidemic of obesity, and diseases related to obesity. Labels such as "No Fat," "Low Fat," "Low Cal," "One Calorie," have been the trend since the 1970's. Look where it has gotten us.

Lets back up to Anatomy 101...

Remember those cells that were dividing perfectly to form the trillions of cells that make up your body today? Well, the outer lining or membrane of every cell in the body is made of lipids... aka...FATS! Therefore, FATS AND OILS ARE VITAL FOR HEALTHY CELLS and HEALTHY CELLS ARE VITAL FOR A HEALTHY BODY. Therefore, it is important that we do not cut fats out of our diet. It is critical, however, that we consume good, or healthy, fats and oils.

Good Fats and Oils

To keep it simple, I avoid cooking with or eat anything but the following fats and oils: Virgin olive oil, Virgin coconut oil, avocado oil, grape seed oil and regular butter (in moderation).
 These are the superstars of good oils.

Olive Oil: Living in Europe, I found it interesting that the grocery stores had entire aisles for certain foods. These were: alcohol, cheese, yogurt, and oils. That says a lot about the dietary 'staples' of the culture.

Here in the US we have entire aisles dedicated to dairy products, chips/snacks, candy/chocolate, breakfast cereals and frozen dinners. Hmm!

In the European oil aisle, there are countless brands of olive oil and virgin olive oil. It is used in everything! Best of all, it is inexpensive. In the states, we have a number of cooking oils available; however, a tiny bottle of healthy olive oil costs a small fortune while a gallon jug of hydrogenated vegetable oil, that easily converts to deadly trans-fatty acids when heated, is quite affordable. Since the first edition of my book olive oil and coconut oil have made an affordable "come back" in the us. Now we are seeing more affordable ways to buy both of these oils in larger quantities as Sam's Club and Costco.

While living in Portugal, my family and I took a drive through the countryside of Spain. We passed through a number of beautiful olive orchards. "Wow," I thought, "I wonder where America grows all the vegetables for the hydrogenated oils Americans typically use…you know the ones…vegetable oil, saffola oil, and the other ones available in one gallon to five gallon jugs for home consumption. (Trans-fatty acids do not occur in nature. They are made by chemically altering a natural product and cooking it at a high temperature.) I wonder why they don't do that here with olive oil. I wonder if that has anything to do with the catastrophic health problems in the US. In the US we produce and ship hydrogenated oils all over the country slowly poisoning people to make a buck." I brought my attention to the road but soon my thoughts wandered again. "Wow, olive oil is so healthy, it's incredibly affordable here in Europe. In America it's $8 for a tiny bottle of olive oil. Why do we charge so much for the healthy stuff and so little for the unhealthy stuff? Is there some great dark company trying to make its millions of dollars at the expense of the health of America?" Then it hit me. There are several "Great Dark Companies" who thrive on making their millions at the expense of the health of our population.

The Next Trillion, a book by Paul Zane Pilzer, points out how we are making a shift away from "disease based health care" to a more "health and prevention" model. He also notes how for some time, we as a world population have been the systematic target of marketing gurus working for junk food manufactures. Their products cause sickness and obesity. The real money has not been in "wellness" but in "sickness." Thus, we have junk-food and medication commercials bombarding our consciousness through TV, billboards, convenient stores, vending machines, etc. The US government subsidizes farmers to grow and distribute the unhealthy oils (and other chemically altered crops) which are a key player in the cause of disease. This, in turn, causes an obese and disease riddled nation in need of "health care" or disease care. Health care or insurance costs skyrocket and we get stuck in the vicious cycle of, "I can't afford to eat healthy and I can't afford health care." This is an entire topic in itself. For now, let's just get back to olive oil…

Olive oil's health benefits

- The beneficial health effects of olive oil are due to both its high content of monounsaturated fatty acids and its high content of antioxidant substances. Studies have shown that olive oil offers protection against heart disease by controlling LDL ("bad") cholesterol levels while raising HDL (the "good" cholesterol) levels. (1-3) No other naturally produced oil has as large an amount of monounsaturated as olive –oil, mainly oleic acid.

- Olive oil is tolerated well by the stomach. In fact, olive oil's protective function has a beneficial effect on ulcers and gastritis. Olive oil activates the secretion of bile and pancreatic hormones much more naturally than prescribed drugs. Consequently, it lowers the incidence of gallstone formation.

- Studies have shown that people who consumed 25 milliliters (mL) - about 2 tablespoons - of virgin olive oil daily for 1 week showed less oxidation of LDL cholesterol and higher levels of antioxidant compounds, particularly phenols, in the blood.[53]

- While all types of olive oil contain monounsaturated fat, EXTRA VIRGIN olive oil, from the first pressing of the olives, contains higher levels of antioxidants, particularly vitamin E and phenols, because it is less processed.

- Olive oil is clearly one of the good oils, one of the healing fats. Most people do quite well with it since it does not upset the critical omega 6 to omega 3 ratios. Most of the fatty acids in olive oil are actually omega-9 oil which is monounsaturated.

Generally, olive oil is extracted by pressing or crushing olives. Olive oil comes in different varieties, depending on the amount of processing involved.

Varieties include:

- **Extra virgin** – considered the best, least processed, comprising the oil from the first pressing of the olives.

- **Virgin** – from the second pressing.

- Pure – undergoes some processing, such as filtering and refining.

- **Extra light** – undergoes considerable processing and only retains a very mild olive flavor.

When buying olive oil, you will want to obtain high quality EXTRA VIRGIN oil. The oil that comes from the first "pressing" of the olive, extracted without using heat (a cold press) or chemicals, and has no "off" flavors, is awarded "extra virgin" status. The less the olive oil is handled, the closer to its natural state, the better the oil. If the olive oil meets all the criteria, it can be designated as "extra virgin".

What is pure and light olive oil? "Pure" olive oil is made by adding a little extra virgin olive oil to refined olive oil. It is a lesser grade oil that is also labeled as just "olive oil" in the U.S.

Olive oil versus Canola oil

Do not fall for the media hype which is put out by traditional medicine regarding the promotion of canola oil (rapeseed) as superior due to its concentration of monounsaturated fatty acids. Olive oil is far superior and has been around for thousands of years. Canola oil is a relatively recent development and the original crops were unfit for human consumption due to their high content of a dangerous fatty acid called euric acid.

If the taste of olive oil is a problem, or if you are frying or sautéing food, then you should consider coconut oil. Many nutritionally misinformed people would consider this unwise due to coconut oil's nearly exclusive content of saturated fat. However, this is not the case. Because it has mostly saturated fat, it is much less dangerous when heated. The heat will not tend to cause the oil to transition into dangerous trans-fatty acids.

Interestingly enough, cattle ranchers discovered the difference between saturated and unsaturated fats in the 1940s, when they fed their livestock inexpensive coconut oil (a saturated fat) in order to fatten them for market. But the cattle didn't gain weight. Instead coconut oil made them lean, active and hungry. Next, ranchers tested a thyroid-suppressing drug. As expected, the livestock gained weight on less food, but because the drug was strongly carcinogenic, it was discontinued. By the late 1940s, ranchers discovered that soybean and corn caused the same anti-thyroid effect as the thyroid-suppressing drug, allowing animals to gain more weight on less food. Since then, corn and soy have been the staples of feedlot cattle.[54]

Coconut Oil: Coconut oil has fantastic health and healing properties. Now there are different ways to process it some of which are toxic. That is why virgin coconut oil that has been processed from fresh coconut meat without chemicals or high heating is the way to go.

Coconut oil developed a bad reputation in the 50's but the assumptions were incorrect. It was simply inappropriately studied, misunderstood, and categorized incorrectly with the bad fats and oils.

- Virgin coconut oil has anti-microbial and anti-viral properties.

- It has medium chain fatty acids (as apposed to un-healthy long chain fatty acids).*

- It has Lauric acid. This is one of the healthy ingredients of human breast milk.

- It is not damaged by heat because it contains no en-zymes. (Remember coconuts can grow in climates natu-rally reaching over 130 degrees)

- It is loaded with healthy saturated fats.

*Coconut oil contains MCTs or medium chain triglycerides. Most vegetable oils are made of longer chain fatty acids, or triglycerides; often called LCTs for short. Here is an important note: LCTs are usually stored in body fat while MCTs are burned for energy. This is very important in metabolism and weight loss.[55]

Bad fats and oils

Basically the vegetable seed oils, especially the hydrogenated or partially hydrogenated oils, are extremely toxic to our bodies. Yes, they make golden crispy French fries, but when heated they produce trans-fatty acids. As stated earlier, trans-fatty acids are not found in nature, they are a byproduct of man-made or chemically altered oil. Our body does not know how to break them down and dispose of them in a healthy way. Thus, they alter our physiology in a harmful way. They are purely toxic. Yet through marketing and misinformation, these oils have become the "norm" in our diet. They are used in homes and restaurants throughout America and are spreading to other parts of the world.

Animal fats are better than the vegetable seed oils but still rank in the "bad fats and oils" category and should be used sparingly.

Man-made chemical compounds produced for their aesthetic qualities such as easy to spread with a knife equal BAD FATS. Margarine is awful! You are far better off using real butter, just watch your portions.

TECHNIQUE FOR ADVANCED LIVING

Fats and Oils:

Remember the outer lining or cell membrane of every cell in the body is made up of lipids (fats and oils). Your body makes 300 Billion new cells every day. It is vital for health and longevity to have GOOD fats and oils as part of your diet.

GOOD stuff:

1. Olive Oil (in the US buy it in bulk, it is much cheaper)

2. Coconut Oil. Fantastic for baking, in fruit smoothies, popcorn, topically for massage, lotion, conditioner, etc.

3. Real Butter (Use it, just don't abuse it)

4. Fish Oil (omega 3) Wild Fish – Salmon, Quality supplement http://www.nutriwest.com/home/index.htm

BAD stuff:

- Corn oil
- Cottonseed oil
- Sunflower oil
- Safflower oil
- Margarine (formerly used as axle grease in WWII) Man-made chemical just one molecule away from plastic. Yuck!

NOTE:

When eating at restaurants remember Fresh "Atlantic" Salmon is a common synonym for "Farm" salmon.

Dairy Products

Milk is regularly touted as a healthy staple of the American diet. Marketing tells us, "Milk! It does a body good!" We are bombarded with this misinformation by the television, at the grocery stores; even health expos often have a booth for a local milk company with a celebrity sponsor. Fact is, cow's milk is extremely taxing to the body and especially to the immune system. Like most things, a little bit isn't going to hurt but the more you avoid cow milk the better off you will be. Though this may be a controversial issue for some, cow milk has several factors we need to look at:

- Cow's milk is genetically designed for cows! Its purpose is to help a baby calf gain FIVE pounds per day.

- Cow's milk contains large proteins that are difficult for the human body to properly digest.

- Lactose is the sugar in cow's milk. Individuals who do not produce Lactase (the enzyme for breaking down Lactose) are unable to digest this sugar making them "Lactose intolerant."

- More people are allergic to cow's milk than any other food product in the world! (Yes, even peanuts.)

- Cow's milk is extremely effective in causing mucus production. Try drinking a glass of milk when you have a cold. Your body quickly begins to produce more mucus. Sinuses fill up you feel terrible. When your immune system is not over-taxed it may not be as obvious.

- Some research has linked cow's milk to ovarian and prostate cancer. Note: our immune system is fighting cancer 24/7. If cow's milk is challenging our immune system we are certainly more prone to viruses, bacteria, and yes…cancer![56]

132

- Vitamin D. Great! Are there other sources without the milk related complications? Sure!

- Calcium. Yes, cow's milk does contain calcium but that does not mean it is a good source from which to intake and digest the calcium. Calcium is best absorbed in an acidic environment, however, milk is a "base" or the opposite of acid, therefore absorbing calcium from milk is next to impossible. Green vegetables remain a better source for calcium intake.[57]

Detoxify

We are exposed to toxins so regularly it becomes important to periodically set aside time and energy to actually "detox." Aside from the other toxins discussed, the average American over the age of 40 years has 5 to 7 pounds of putrefied red meat stuck in their colon. This not only blocks the proper absorption of nutrients and re-absorption of water in the digestive track, but is extremely toxic.

Like a sponge mop, as it encounters various dirt and partials on the floor, our body becomes saturated with filth.

Over time and with multiple exposures to 'filth' or toxins our body can, like the sponge mop, become saturated.

This can happen gradually, making us unaware of the build-up until it gets to extreme levels.

When we clean a floor we might use a mop and a bucket of water. The mop absorbs grime, and then we wring it out in the bucket of water, sponge, ridding it of the accumulated dirt. Gradually, the bucket of clean water becomes dirty, thus affecting how clean the sponge can become.

The same is true with our body. We can make certain nutritional and physical changes while taking in plenty of pure water, thus "squeezing" or flushing out a great number of toxins. Once we start that change, it becomes noticeable how much better we feel, or how much more energy (mentally, spiritually, and physically) we have.

Fasting is a good example of making changes in a diet type and it helps purge the body of toxins. There are different types of fasts. They all consist of a short-term limitation of ingestible items.

Some religions fast for 24 hours at a time with no food or water to exercise mind/spiritual domination over physical appetites. This is a healthy habit to practice periodically for the following benefits:

- Exercise mind over body control.

- Physically it helps to purge the body of a limited number of toxins.

- Physically it puts the body in "starvation mode" and changes the set-point of the metabolism.

Periodically, a fast of this nature is quite healthy. If practiced too frequently it is not healthy. Fasting of this nature for several days is not recommended. I have spoken with several individuals who regularly skip breakfast extending the *sleep-fast* period from the time we are sleeping to well into their day. Eating soon after we awake is important. That is why it is called, "break fast." Many individuals will skip breakfast because they feel they don't have the time or because they struggle with weight and think it will help to simply eat less. Those who struggle with keeping their weight down and have the habit of eating infrequently need to understand that skipping meals affects the metabolism set-point putting the body in starvation mode. Starvation mode utilizes as few nutrients and calories as possible while the body stores all the calories it can for an emergency...calorie storage is FAT.

An intense fast once or twice per year is a good way to cleans tissues and purge the body of toxins. For example, a three day or ten day "Fruit Fast." In this scenario a person eats all the fresh fruit they want and drinks plenty of pure water. This can really "wring out" deeply stored toxins.

A fruit fast or fruit and vegetable cleanse is quite healthy and can be done regularly throughout the year. A fruit and vegetable cleanse mildly more intense than being a "vegetarian." An individual can practice vegetarianism for as long as they want. Eating fruit alone should not exceed 10 days. Eating fruit and vegetables alone with no grains or nuts should be limited as well. Up to three days of either fast can be done often. Ten days or longer should only be done with the right combination of other healthy nutrients. A true fruit fast for any length of time should only be once or twice per year.

There are numerous types of cleanses. Liver cleanse, colon cleanse, full body detox. You can do more research on the various methods and specifics. Personally, I like to keep it simple for myself and my patients. The fruit fast, or the fruit and vegetable fast, is not complicated.

A good product to help with cleansing can be found at www. drnatura.com. Utilizing the Dr. Natura products while continuing with a somewhat normal diet, may be easier for individuals with diabetes. Note: The Dr. Natura products are more effective the closer your daily diet is to a "vegan" diet.

The Following Cleanse suggestions are rated "Gold, Silver, and Bronze" days. Gold is the most cleaning. If it is too difficult, try bumping yourself to the Silver menu.

Still too tough? Try the Bronze menu.

They are all good for you. If you have a 10-day goal, try to squeeze in as many "Gold" days as possible. It is no problem to have a few "Silver or Bronze" days in the mix. Good Luck!

DR. SHETLIN'S TEN-DAY CLEANSE

Gold Star Day: All the fresh fruits and vegetables you can eat. Plenty of water. Natural "Green Drinks" not the ones containing sugar.

Be creative with "smoothies." In the blender add ½ cup of fresh squeezed orange juice one banana, some frozen strawberries or other frozen mixed fruit, 2 or 3 baby carrots, and some "green drink powder" or some leafy spinach.

Vegetables through the day can be raw or steamed.

Silver Star Day: All the fresh fruits and vegetables you can eat. Plenty of water. Natural "Green Drinks" **not** the ones containing sugar or High Fructose Corn Syrup. Small amounts of nuts or trail mix (without sugar or candy like M&M's). Almond or Rice milk. Virgin olive oil and virgin coconut oil (http://www. drjayshetlin.com/resources.php)

Again, smoothies are great! Just a touch of vanilla Almond milk really adds to the flavor and provides some protein. A tablespoon of virgin coconut cream is fantastic in the smoothies as well. Coconut oil will work but with frozen fruit or cold temperatures it will granulate leaving a gritty texture. Coconut cream works perfect!

Virgin coconut oil or cream can be taken a tablespoon in the morning, everyday. Just take it straight if you can handle the taste. If you can work up to taking in 3 tablespoons a day either in your smoothies, cooking with it or taking it straight it will be very beneficial.

Nibbling on some trail mix through the day will help satisfy mild hunger with good proteins and fats.

With the oils you can make healthy salad dressings to flavor up all the vegetables you are eating. Spices and herbs are fine to use to add flavor.

Bronze Star Day: All the fresh fruits and vegetables you can eat. Plenty of water. Natural "Green Drinks" not the ones containing sugar. Small amounts of nuts or trail mix (without sugar or candy like M&M's). Almond or Rice milk. Virgin olive oil and virgin coconut oil (http://www.drjayshetlin.com/resources.php or www.tropicaltraditions.com). Real butter in small quantities. Some pasta, grains, and oats.

Same as the above days but you can add things like malt-o-meal, oatmeal for breakfast and pasta with vegetables for lunch and dinner. This may be the low day of our three choices, but it remains a nutritional day, far better than the average American diet.

Vanilla rice milk and almond milk are great on morning cereal…oatmeal, malt-o-meal, granola, fiber, etc.

Look up some vegetarian recipes on-line or check out a cookbook. There are many fantastic vegetarian recipes with pasta that are delicious.

Sweeteners: Use only Honey, Fruit, and real Fructose (from the health food store) if possible, organic brown sugar. NOTE: Fructose looks like table sugar (sucrose) but is sweeter, requires less and is better for your body.

NOTE: With a cleanse type diet they are high in carbs (loaded with fruits and vegetables). This is not a fat-burn diet. For that you need low carb-low fat with plenty of protein. I just want you to understand the purpose of the 3 day and 10 day cleanse diets are just that… a cleanse. If you have the energy, you can work out while doing the cleanse.

When you start "the cleanse," the second and third day are usually the most difficult. Your body is changing gears and adapting. Sometimes you may feel like you can't get full. Eat all the fresh fruits and veggies you want. If you continue to struggle to feel full, drop down to the "Silver Star" plan. The longer you can stay on the "Gold Star" plan the better but all of these days are fantastic dietary habits so don't feel guilty using any of them.

When you are finishing up with your cleanse, ease back into other foods. Don't go out for a big steak, potato and cream pie the last day or you will feel awful! I am not just saying that. Your body is very adaptive and it changes gears to this lighter, healthier diet. You will feel it if you bombard your digestive system with heavy proteins, creams, and sugars after it has shifted gears to the healthier diet. It is a pretty clear sign of how we should be eating all the time.

Fair warning: If you are really toxic there may be "detox symptoms" such as a headache. It will pass once the toxins are flushed out. Water, water, water.

Have fun with your cleanse!

TECHNIQUE FOR ADVANCED LIVING

Get the right amount of healthy building blocks for your body type. "Over nutrition" or too many of the wrong calories slowly leads to an early, death.

Eat Smart:

1. Know your daily caloric requirements

2. Try to average thirds or 40%, 30%, 30% - carbohydrates, fats and proteins with snack or meal.

3. Eat 10-12 servings per day of fruits and vegetables. If you aren't... supplement!

4. Avoid inflammatory, clogging and mucus forming foods (the wrong fats, dairy, excessive red meat)

5. Cleanse periodically – Fast 1x per month

Or – Pure Fruit fast only
for a few days 2-3 times per year.

– Fruit and Veggie fast for up to 10 days at a time several times through the year.

– Vegetarian – with nuts and grains, go as long as you want.

Footnotes:

53. References for Olive oil:

   Keys A, Menotti A, Karvonen MJ, et al: The Diet and 15-year Death Rate in the Seven Countries Study Am J Epidemiol 124; 903-915 (1986)

   Willett Wc: Diet and Coronary Heart Disease Monographs in Epidemiology and Biostatistics 15: 341-379 (1990)

   World Health Organization: Diet, nutrition, and the prevention of chronic diseases. Report of the WHO Study Group. WHO Technical Report Series 797, Geneva 1990

   European Journal of Clinical Nutrition April 2002;56:114-120

54. http://www.naturalhealthstrategies.com/coconut-oil-and-weight-loss-cows.html

55. Coconut Oil Book www.TropicalTraditions.com

56. ScienceDaily (Aug. 5, 2005) - An analysis of 21 studies that have investigated the link between ovarian cancer and the consumption of milk products and lactose has found some support for the hypothesis that high intake is associated with increased cancer risk. The results of this analysis, published online August 5, 2005 in the International Journal of Cancer, the official journal of the international Union Against Cancer (UICC), found the support was strong in cohort studies, compared to case-control studies, which offered varying results. The article is available via Wiley Inter-Science at Http://www.interscience.wiley.com/journal/ijcd

57. http://nutritionfacts.org/video/plant-vs-cow-calcium-2/

HARRISON • PART IV

The day we drove home from our pediatrician's office when Harrison was 2 months old, I knew Harrison would be alright. Although my definition of "alright" may be different than others, I knew deep-down that Harrison would be able to overcome his balance and equilibrium challenges due to the Cerebral Palsy. What I didn't know was how long it would take, but that didn't matter. What had been impressed upon my mind was to "do what I knew is best (parent's intuition combined with my medical training) and be patient." Just before moving back to the States, I took the kids to a local park to play the ever-popular European game of soccer. While his brothers and sister ran around the grass, laughing, playing and kicking the ball, three-and-a-half-year-old Harrison did something amazing: He ran out to join them, kicking a soccer ball around the field! Though his form wasn't perfect, it was nothing shy of miraculous.

As I write this book in 2016, Harrison is now 14 years old. At 12 years old I helped him write his own book, "The Boy Who Would Never Run." Today you can't tell any difference between him and his peers. His story is close to my heart because he is my son. But there are literally thousands of stories, like Harrison's, of people who have overcome physical difficulties through the right "recipe." Male or female, young or old the right recipe for success in health is simply, the right blueprints (nerve flow), the right building blocks (nutrition) and avoiding toxins. Add in some physical stimuli (exercise) it is better still. Regardless of your religious background, when you add some faith into the mix, you have an even better recipe for success. The questions are, simply: How long will it take? and Are you patient enough to stick to the recipe?

A story of hope and perseverance in overcoming life's challenges

Harrison
The Boy Who Would Never Run

by Harrison Shetlin
with Dr. R. Jay Shetlin

FINANCES

It is important to have a brief and focused financial portion in this book because money matters are at the top of the list of things we think about and possibly stress over. Since THOUGHTS directly affect our health and well-being, having some financial stress-reducing tips may serve to decrease our anxiety overall and thus reduce the negative effect on our physiology.

There are countless ways to make money, save money, invest for retirement or protect your future assets. It is sound advice for every family to have a financial advisor they can afford. I would like to simply share a few basic points and then share an interview on health and wealth with Financial Guru, Garrett Gunderson, author of *"Killing Sacred Cows."*

Across the Globe

I have been blessed with the opportunity to not only travel but live in diverse parts of the world and truly gain an understanding of people, cultures, habits and varying views of life.

The American pattern – Live large! We strive, as the saying goes, "to keep up with the Joneses." Oft times we try to 'out do' the Jones'. Most Americans live beyond their means throughout their prime

143

income earning years, saving little or nothing for their future. The average American saves less than 2% of their annual income. In 2008 our national average was *a negative 2%* so we really spent more than we made. (Growth rate: 2.3 children per couple.[58])

We are constantly pushing for the bigger better house, the nicer car, a closet full of shoes, the latest electronic gadgets. Americans are status driven, usually living beyond their means; buying things now on credit because we want instant gratification and we'll worry about paying for it later. That is exactly what causes "worry" — a negative emotion yielding stress to our mental, spiritual and physical faculties. To minimize this stress we work longer, eat processed and fast food so we can get back to whatever it is we believe is more important, as quickly as possible. Hurry to work, hurry to eat, hurry to recreate with the family so we can hurry back to the cycle. America is a rushed, debt-based society, which is fundamentally stressful and unhealthy.

The Asian Pattern – Live a humble existence and save 20% to 27% of your annual income. Children and the elderly are respected (much more so than in the West). These age groups are cared for by the middle-aged. These individuals work hard to provide for their children's education, and work to develop their children's talents. The elderly are either well prepared for retirement or at least have a home/land for the family to live on as they are supported by their middle-aged children. (Large families are uncommon.[59])

The European Pattern – Life is for living. Work, and live within your means. Save for the future 8% to 12%, spend quality time with friends and family, enjoy frequent holidays and take the month of August off for vacation. (Growth rate has been declining since 2004. Some countries have only 0.6 children per couple.[60])

The Basics

There are many generalized examples to show some of the strengths and weaknesses of varying cultures. All have good and bad traits. The simplest advice is this:

- Live within your means, it will greatly reduce stress.
- Give 10% of your gross income to your church or the charities of your choosing.
- Give 10 % of your gross income to yourself, investing in your future and retirement.
- Budget. Do not simply fly by the seat of you pants every paycheck.
- Invest in yourself and your health, you are your number one asset.

We have talked about the Law of Attraction; now let's discuss a portion of the Law of Sacrifice. This law dwarfs the Law of Attraction in many ways and has a much deeper meaning than what will be discuss within these pages. In this chapter we will merely touch on the Law of Sacrifice in a financial realm.

Put simply, "We must give to get."

35% Housing	20% Transportation	20% Other
Spend no more than 35% of net income on housing. That includes: mortgage or rent, utilities, insurance, taxes and home maintenance.	Spend no more than 20% of net income on transportation. That includes: car payments, auto insurance, tag or license, maintenance, gasoline and parking.	Spend no more than 20% of net income on all other expenses: food, clothing, entertainment, child care, medical expenses, tithing and charity.

We sacrifice or give our time and talents to our family in order to 'get' or raise good, healthy, balanced children.

We sacrifice or give our time and talents to our job in order to receive a paycheck.

We are naturally better off when we give back or return to God/the Universe a portion of what we have been given. This is directly related to both the Law of Sacrifice and Gratitude from the first chapter.

The Judeo-Christian faiths might refer to paying yourself and your God FIRST as, "Tithing." Call it what you want. For some people paying tithing is easy. Others have difficulty separating themselves from their worldly assets. The most common mistake is NOT paying these two first, but rather waiting until after other bills and obligations are paid, then trying to tithe to your charity and your future with what is left over. This plan has a high failure rate.

15% Debt	**10% Savings**
Spend no more than 15% of net income on debt: student loans, retail installment contracts, credit cards, personal loans, tax debs and medical debts.	Save at least 10% of income throughout your working life.

Pay Yourself First

Physically "pay yourself first" by taking care of your body. Your health is your number one asset. Without your health your ability to earn income, provide for yourself and your family, donate a portion of your time or money to charities…these are all diminished.

Financially "pay yourself first" by putting 10% into investments that will payoff for you over time. Quick return usually means greater risk or even loss. Be the tortoise, not the hare, when it comes to your investments.

Money in a local bank savings account at 0.5% to 1.5% is like flushing money down the toilet. The bank is making money off of your money. With the inflation rate averaging 4% over the last 30 years, your savings / investments need to yield greater than 4% or you are losing money.

To take it from here I would like to introduce Mr. Garrett Gunderson, hands down one of the most gifted financial advisor I have had the pleasure of meeting in my life. His "New Rules to Get Rich" program address the **FIVE pillars to true wealth**. These five pillars are so much more balanced and fulfilling than simply having financial wealth.

Garrett B. Gunderson — Transcription

Dr. Shetlin interview with Garret Gunderson – Financial Advisor and author of *"Killing Sacred Cows."*

SHETLIN: What is true wealth and what are the 5 pillars of wealth?

GUNDERSON: To some, being rich means to have a lot of money. But that does not necessarily constitute wealth in my world because there are miserable millionaires and there are broke millionaires. There is a whole philosophy for a lot of people that if they never spend their money that they can accumulate a whole bunch of it so they can become a millionaire. But that's just dots on a piece of paper.

So, I think money is important. If someone says it's not important, they probably either don't have very much of it or they're not going to have a lot because the things that we don't find important, we typically don't have a lot of.

I think money is a lot like air, if you have plenty of it, then its no big deal. But if not, it's pretty suffocating.

I would say that money is one track or pillar of being wealthy. But there are really these four other tracks that are critically important. And one of the core philosophies or principles that we have has to do with living wealthy not just having wealth. I call the first one, "Soul purpose."

"Soul purpose" is a combination of someone's passions, their values, their abilities combined for a great intention or purpose in their life. When we are engaged in our soul purpose, we feel fulfilled. We feel excited. It's going to elicit more passion. It's going to engage our best abilities. And so, that's definitely part of being wealthy.

There is also, "Mindset." There is a "Mental track." Because if someone had a great deal of money but always feared losing it or always thought everyone was out to get them, or didn't have any way to enjoy or spend it, that is what I would call a "scarcity or "poverty mindset." That's going to limit them in feeling wealthy.

SHETLIN: So we have what some would call, "Mental Capital" or a healthy-wealthy way of thinking that attracts positive things, even wealth. I would call that an "abundance mindset." Some people have a "poverty mindset" where they lack the mental capital to attract because they are constantly in fear of losing what they have or afraid to put in the proper effort to gain anything beyond what they already have.

GUNDERSON: Yes. One of the next pillars, of which you are an expert in, Dr. Shetlin, is really physical health. If people don't have their health, it's really hard to be wealthy because it's not really enjoyable when someone is always sick, or in pain, or deteriorating, in some way shape or form or has low energy. So, taking care of one's self is absolutely important to being wealthy.

148

And the fifth piece is the, "Social track." The Social tract demonstrates that people are really the only assets. It is about relationships, it's about vacations, it's about rejuvenation, it is about having an enjoyable life along the way.

Simply put, there are five tracts to balanced wealth: Finance, Soul purpose, Mental, Physical, and Social. If you are strong in all five of those tracks, then I think you are wealthy. That's true wealth.

If you only have one of those track working for you or even if you have one that isn't working for you, think about it, if you have no social life what's so ever, or, trouble in marriage, or something like that, all those areas don't have as much enjoyment, purpose or fulfillment because it really starts to drain energy and bleeds over.

Shetlin: Understanding this is powerful for ALL individuals but even more instrumental for a business owner.

Your Greatest Asset

GUNDERSON: The philosophy is that you are your greatest access. You have to invest in yourself. What I mean by that is it's back to the premise of mindset. You can have a whole bunch of money but if you don't feel wealthy and you are feeling, "scarcity" or "poverty stricken," none of that really matters as much. But if you invest in yourself it's about taking care of those five tracks.

It all starts with beginning your day with intention. And you know I talk about something called the "power hour," Dr. Shetlin, you call it, "Techniques for advanced living," where you start with some exercise. That's going to release endorphins; it's going to create a healthier environment for energy.

Second is education. This is finding that area where you can increase your expertise and study it. Actually feeding yourself that way so you can advance in what you're doing.

Third, is enlightenment. What I'm talking about is spiritual discipline that leads towards, peace of mind, that leads towards clarity, that leads towards connection, and so, for some that might be prayer or scripture reading. To others it might be mediation. Others still, it might be taking a walk or sitting down and listing out the things they are grateful for. So, I'm not here to tell people what it is for them, I 'm here to just give that idea and construct it.

If you invest in yourself on a daily basis, you show up more proactively and more powerfully throughout the day.

Now, we have to question what "investing" is because most people think investing is synonymous with putting your money in the stock market.

Most people put their money in the market and they hope it works out for them in 30 years. But unfortunately it has not worked out like it is supposed to. Yet that is what people are doing every single day because they don't know anything different. But if we look at investing as creating value, the most important piece is to create value for yourself first, so you have enough to give, so you have the best expression of who you are. If investing starts to deteriorate personal fulfillment, where it starts to create concern and worry...For example:

Let's say someone says, "Hey! You really need to start dealing in some real estate." You get involved in a piece of real estate. But you didn't know a lot about it. It wasn't that exciting to you. But you thought, well I really should because I can start making money. You start losing sleep. Or it starts creating stress. You as a doctor might not be as productive from day to day because of that outside stress. It might start to become a distraction.

So, investing to me, first of all, is taking care of yourself!

Secondly, is saying, what am I doing and does it align with "value creation?" My own personal knowledge? Do I know why it would earn a rate of return, or why it would benefit me? And I would say, before you even get to putting dollars towards something like that, do the three "E's"... because they don't take money...

Exercise,

Education

and

Enlightenment,

they just take time…right? It is building a foundation.

SHETLIN: Yes, these are similar to the "Techniques of Advanced Living" I teach my patients. How to start the day right so they are more productive energized and have less stress through the day.
   GUNDERSON: Right.

And whether you are a business owner, or whether you are a W-2 employee, you've got to get six months' expenses saved up.

You know, it's a, "Piece of mind fund." It's kind of like insurance in that you don't know what could happen. You could have a family member get sick. You could have some kind of catastrophic event. I really think that there are surprises that happen in life. But most of them don't have to be surprises financially if you have the right structure.

You build the foundation of security and safety first.

So you get that liquidity built up in a savings account.

You should go through and make sure you have the right coverages with insurance. Do you have the right car insurance? Home owner's insurance? Liability insurance? Do you have disability insurance policies? It's probably going to be critically important as a business owner. That said, as a Chiropractor for example, you had to spend a lot of money to become a Chiropractor, so if you have the right disability policy, even if you can't adjust people, but you can teach then you can still get coverage to bridge the income gap until you perfect a different line of work.

You want to have your medical insurance, your life insurance, your business owner policies, etc., having all of that foundationally handled. This relieves a great deal of stress and worry (i.e. changes the focus of the mental tract and frees up more mental capital for growth and prosperity in the other tracts).

I think this is the first step for everyone in their finances, then you start looking at investing.

But here is the thing, business owner, or W-2 employee, why not invest in stable things to start with? Predictable things... think more about return of your money, then on return on your money. Because far too many people are very aggressive in those dollars, not knowing it, they think they are in a Mutual Fund that are diversified but, in fact, is a growth fund so, it is in stocks and it has volatility meaning it goes up and down. With volatility the investor's emotions go up and down with it a lot of times.

What if you were to invest in things that are more predictable? Maybe invest in things you know or things you are confident are more stable. Maybe like municipal bonds, or guaranteed insurance contracts? Something that provides more stability.

If that is a big chunk of what you have invested, especially as a W-2 person and putting that in more stable investments. After that you can take a small portion of your money, on top of that, and if you want to be more speculative and then that might be something that you go to the Stock Market, that would be a safer way to invest. Or if you want to invest in real estate knowing that it isn't going to be your main area of expertise, now it's only a small chunk of your investment funds vs. using all of your investment funds in something volatile or unpredictable. That leaves less of your money at risk.

If we analyze that, over decades, over lifetimes...it far out performs. There's a book called "Anti-Fragile", written by the same person that did the "Black Swan," and that book talks about the allocations most people have in their portfolios are far too risky. And if they actually do the opposite, which is only taking a small piece... it's a long book and a lot of pages to say what I just said in a pretty short period of time.

But as a business owner, don't speculate anything outside of your business.

Put your speculation in your business. If you make a mistake, you can learn from it. An investment in business is people, process and procedure. And procedure to me is like automated technology, its things that don't require ongoing human labor. Process is ongoing human labor knowing what sequences in order to do it, and people...get the very best team so it's not always about you doing all the work. So, that would be an investment in business!

Then keep everything else stable and fairly liquid so you don't have to mess around with commodities, the real estate market, options trading, foreign exchange, and all of this stuff that's confusing and causes people to lose money. And I think if people would really consider that, they would find themselves far better off in the long run.

There is a company that you may be familiar with, "Whitehall." They were big in Chiropractic and dentistry (coaching) for decades. We find people that worked with them ten years ago, twenty years ago, and they were typically a wealthier group of people. They were just paying-off debts and putting money in bonds. Everyone was saying, "the Stock Market averaged ten percent over 30 years." Yet I'm looking at the actually numbers and I'm wondering, "why are these people so much more successfully then everyone that just threw all their money into a 401k and the stock market." Because volatility and fees, and averages versus actual returns. I cover a lot of this topic inside my the book, "Killing Sacred Cows." Look, a lot of it is marketing instead of reality.

SHETLIN: Before I started learning the philosophies you are talking about I would work in practice and stress over where to invest for retirement, how do I buy the right stocks? should I invest in property? The more I became distracted with that, the more I became distracted from my practice, patients and community. But when I brought my focus back to family-practice and patients, my practice thrived.

GUNDERSON: No one understands until they experience it. "A double dip." A double dip is, in economics, it's usually talking about a market that goes down, and down again beyond what you thought it was going to be. But, in losing in an investment, the investment goes down, but the mentality of the person, their personal confidence, their attention to other things more productive, so, it's not just the loss in the investments it's the loss of productivity of the individual that's not measured or reported that it actually the much more significant loss.

SHETLIN: From an individual perspective, so many of us are chasing wealth in our youth but then flush most of our savings in our older years trying to regain the health we squandered on the road to financial gain. How would you address this issue?

GUNDERSON: This is a philosophical issue. Philosophically, people would have you believe that the way to be wealthy is directly related to the amount of money you save, how early you started to save it, and how much risk you took on that money to get a return. That's what most people believe.

So now what happens, is people start making decisions on whether they should take their money and invest it into a product that is supposed to grow for 30 years, or should they take it an invest it in more knowledge around their health, or more health benefits beyond just insurance? Because to me, insurance is a very reactive type of structure. It gets people to address what is covered, not what is important or necessarily. This is even a mindset that people have fallen into with their investments.

154

To me, you have to look at the priority of, okay, if I'm my greatest asset, what's more important, taking the best care of my health today because I'm the one that can be productive? Or putting my money into an account that gets automatic fees taking out of it that I don't even understand, that I'm supposed to benefit when I turn age 65 or 30 years from now, whichever is longer? I may do that at the expense of maybe eating healthier. Why? Because I've been told hey it's just too expensive to eat healthy. So I know that I can get really cheap food for a dollar, but at the same time it's deteriorating my health and I am going to have to address that in the future. Or, if I could just work harder now and longer hours, then I could take that extra money and sock it away so I could have a better retirement. So, at the cost of my living wealth today, out of my long term health, because now maybe the stress creates higher blood pressure for me. Maybe not going and getting adjusted, now all of a sudden I have all these issues going on that are going to have long term effects because I don't address them today. Not eating healthy enough…then all of a sudden it puts more stress on my body and maybe now… Actually, Doc, you could go into all the science beyond what I'm talking about here.

But, it's very unfortunate, because it is true; it's a saying because it's happen so often. People accumulate piles of money, and then they spend it in 2 to 3 years in their retired years on hospital care, and hospice, medications, and transplants…all of these kinds of things. And that's when it was supposed to be the golden years where they got to enjoy life. They missed out on their best years of life to differ to a time where they were afraid to spend their money and that extra stress starts to kill them.

So, when it comes to a health decision, I don't really put a budget or a cap on those health decisions. If it's going to be a right thing for me to be healthier, I know that I'm going to be more productive, I'm going to think more clearly, I'm going to feel better about myself,

I look at it as an investment instead of a cost. Most people look at it as a cost.

And they weight the cost and in the way they've been taught which is, how do I minimize my cost?

Classifying Costs

But here's the way you've got to classify that… There are different types of costs. There are some costs that are expensive because they are destructive. Right? I'm pretty sure Heroine is always destructive. Or it could be candy for someone that's addicted to sweets. Or, alcohol for an alcoholic. These are destructive expenses or costs.

Then there are consumptive expenses or costs which might be: I want to go on a nice trip to Italy. Or I want to go vacation to Hawaii. That pretty consumptive. It is not necessarily benefiting my business, but at the same time, it feels good, it is something I enjoy. It is a reward for me. Don't borrow for those things. Just pay cash for that kind of stuff.

Then, there are protective expenses or costs. For me, being proactive with wellness, that is a protective expense or cost for me. I may not feel differently tomorrow from it…I may not notice a major different this week, but I know by adoption this lifestyle, by having liquidity in my savings account, by getting regular adjustments, by going to a medical institute once a year or a retreat, where I'm really going through and learning what's going on, reading books, and time for just a week to myself. That is a protective expense.

It is also a productive expense because I'm feeling better, but it's not usually a symptomatic situation for me. What I have to look at, though, is if I take care of my health, it becomes a productive expense. Because what about the time lost ten years from now when I neglected something. Because now I'm dealing with surgeries, or dealing with medications that have affects that are negative too and I'm dealing with being scared about the situation. I mean, if people could really see that far ahead and just think about, it becomes a very productive expense because now, I'm in better health now than I was 10 years ago even though I was in my twenties ten years ago because I didn't understand what health was. I wasn't investing in education. I wasn't investing in regular Chiropractic care. I wasn't investing in going to this health institute, but once I did, you know what…I feel better. I have more energy. I'm able to actually do more and I'm not facing some of the issues that other people my age and older are normally facing because I was able to be proactive with it.

I don't let my financial life diminish my health. I don't say, "I can't afford it." I say, "what would it take to afford it. How can I make this a priority? And what would happen if I took care of it long term."

And those questions change how people feel about that. You know, there are people that will say, "Well, I can't come in under regular care because we are saving up for Disneyland." It's like, you're finding a way to make Disneyland work, what would it take to find a way a way to make this work for you in your life? You know.

Typically, people just don't ask those questions. There too easily giving in to an excuse. And if you want the results, that most of the world is getting right now which is sickness and obesity, you know, go ahead and have no question, and just say: I can't afford it. But if you want to have results of the people that live life at the best level, and that are moving towards health instead of sickness, you have to ask yourself: what would it take? How can I make this a priority? What benefit would this give me now and in the future? And you can't live just upon symptoms because people don't make investing decisions that way and go: "Oh well the market is going down today so I am going to 'cash out' and then tomorrow I'm going back in." That's a bit erratic. Investors usually have a longer term philosophy and they don't look at it as an expense, they look at it as an investment. So look at your health as an investment instead of an expense.

SHETLIN: I hear people all the time say, "I can't afford it." Or they say, "If my insurance doesn't cover then I can't afford it." They literally transfer that responsibility of their own health to someone else.

GUNDERSON: But they don't say that they can't afford to eat. They don't say that they can't buy clothes. They find money for "priorities." For some reason, in our world, if we don't feel sick we think we can't afford it. If tomorrow they knew that the care they received today would prevent cancer, the whole conversation would change. I think half of it is due to bad habits handed down from generation to generation combined with a lack of education.

SHETLIN: Thanks. That is very enlightening on that topic.
You brought up chiropractic. Obviously, I am a doctor of chiropractic and I love what I do. You love what you do. How were you first introduced to chiropractic?

GUNDERSON: I went to Dr. Craig Buhler when I was running in my twenties. My feet were going numb and someone referred me to him. I didn't know that he was a doctor of Chiropractic, I just heard here is someone that could help and he did. He helped me quickly, within 3 weeks. But he sold me on this process of maximized benefit and maximized potential with your health. And so, I bought into this concept of wellness and started seeing a Chiropractor closer to my house for a long time…someone I think you know.

Then I happened to meet Dr. Patrick Gemtempo, who owned Chiropractic Leadership Alliance. He told me about a program called, "Total Solution." At that same time, we were having stress with our son and some health issues he was having. My wife pointed out some of his challenges and I began to see what she was talking about. At the same time, he was put into a special education program. Around then is when we met Patrick, he invited us to Total Solutions and I brought my wife along.

See, I would have certain notions that seem crazy to people… like, "Yeah, I don't think we should vaccinate" and, "I think that we should eat this certain kinds of food." But I didn't have the science behind it, it was just intuition. It's like when you reading an article that made sense to me. I was somewhat of a fact finder. So we went to Total Solutions, my wife really got the science behind things. When we had our first child, he was a little colicky and I said, "let's take him to get adjusted." "Adjusted?" She thought, "He's an infant." Now I convinced her after a few days of him crying and it really helped out! She's was like, "wow!" But, still there wasn't enough science for her to keep that going regularly until we went to Total Solution. Then a Chiropractor, by the name of Dr. Grayson, helped us find a Chiropractor close to home to specifically help my son with some cranial sacral issues. They also helped us find a nutritionist and another Chiropractor that tested for all sorts of chemicals that we were being exposed to. They checked for any metal toxicity, and if we needed Chelation. It was like this really comprehensive experience. But our son went from special education to now he is on a four grade reading level in third grade. You know, they introduced us to brain specialists.

Chiropractic is not this skeptical world where they think, "if it's not in a form of a pill, then it can't help you." Instead, they go: "Here is what we can do, and here are some other people we know that do certain specific things." So they introduced us to all sorts of really cool situations! I'm probably the one in my family that gets regular chiropractic the least often. Everyone else gets pretty regular care. I get adjusted by several Chiropractors, because I hang out with so many great docs. But my family is really consistent and it's made a huge difference for us.

And so, it's interesting for me, just like in the world of finance, with investing so commonly thought of as "stocks;" health is so commonly thought of as, "pills."

But, in the world of insurance, when I was 19 years old, I got life insurance license and I was selling life insurance. I learned that if you wanted to get the best rating from a life insurance company, you couldn't be on any medication. So, if it's so good for our health, why at the same time are our insurance companies saying you are at a higher risk because of the meds, not just because of the little bit higher blood pressure, or not just because of the little bit higher cholesterol, that wasn't as much the trigger as if you whether you were on medication for it because I think they understand the effects of it. So, I really like that Chiropractic was more open to what's possible…we don't know everything and have every specific answer but what we do know is that there are some very natural ways to take care of things. You know, we're going to look at how we can do this in the most non-evasive way and then make it more about wellness rather than just being reactive and I really love that philosophy and love spending time with people that are really passionate about those things.

SHETLIN: Garrett, Thank-you for sharing with us not only on financial topics but health. I love the five pillars and how those give us true wealth.

Take Control[61]

YOU CANNOT CONTROL	BUT YOU CAN CONTROL
Social Security	Cash for retirement
Your employer	Alternate sources of income
Taxes	Ways to reduce your taxes
Inflation	Maximizing your investment potential
Rising costs	Saving more
The risk of a single investment	Diversity of your investment choices

By paying yourself before your bills you recapture control of your outcomes. By paying God/the Universe first, you express gratitude, abundance and sacrifice that attract those very principles back to you. Let's be clear, God doesn't need your money, this exercise is for you.

"You cannot solve the problems of today with the same level of thinking that created them." – Albert Einstein

This applies to any principle including heath and wealth principles.

Here are some lessons learned from my "school of hard knocks. This may save you and your family some costly mistakes.

The public perception of doctors is that they are "made of money." People rarely calculate the following: time sacrificed and the strain on a family to study for 8+ years; the enormous student loan debt; the high overhead involved in running a practice; the expense of keeping current on health and medical advances to maintain a license, especially when striving to excel as a physician and not just be mediocre.

With that said, I am quite protective of the money I bring home, *as each of us should be.* When planning and saving for our future we all need to avoid "financial predators," which prey on our hard earned money and believe me, they are out there!

Fatherly Advice

Much like Robert Kiyosaki, the author of "Rich Dad, Poor Dad," I too had a rich dad and a poor dad from which to learn some life lessons. Though the story I am going to share starts while I was in graduate school, the advice from my rich dad has always been:

- "Owning a home is the first step toward building wealth."
- "Protect your family and your assets."
- "Let your money work for **you** not someone else."

Regrettably, I did not know how to apply some of these principles correctly in my earlier years.

While still in Chiropractic College and clearly naive in vital financial matters, a friend from school referred me to a gentleman whom he had done business with to help me start saving for my future while protecting my family with life insurance.

We were renting at the time with no plans of staying in Davenport, Iowa after college; therefore, purchasing a home was not a priority. However, life insurance and saving for the future were.

Applying Rich Dad's:
Advice Protecting Your Famiy & Assets

For a young family, even if you do not own your home yet, life insurance is a wise investment and it shows responsibility.

- If you are a renter it shows banks when you are ready to buy your home that you are thinking ahead and are responsible.
- The younger you start the less expensive it is.

TERM insurance is definitely the way to go for most families, young or old. You can get far more coverage for less monthly cost and overall expense which frees up funds to apply toward a house and retirement.

That said, let me make a disclaimer. There are special types of whole-life plans, that, if setup and managed properly, you can use to your advantage by becoming your own banker. This is an interesting concept since you can build your own bank, so to speak, have it leveraged or protected with life insurance, loan yourself your own money to buy necessities such as a car. This is powerful because you will be making the interest on that loan yourself rather than paying it to some other institution. Like any investment vehicle this requires understanding and discipline.

Graph compliments of Primerica Financial Services

Applying Rich Dad's Advice: Owning Your Home

Owning your home (one within your means) is one of the best wealth building tools available. A few reasons include:

- Equity in your home gives you powerful financial leverage. (Be careful to use it wisely)

- Your home should increase in value by roughly 8% each year or double in value every 10 to 12 years.

- <u>On-time</u> mortgage payments seriously boost your credit scores. (Caution: even a single late payment will cripple your credit scores).

- Banks look at home owners differently than renters. Your home gives you more banking leverage.

- Owning your home offers some personal piece of mind and security.

- Try to stay **put**. Most Americans sell their home and move every 5 to 7 years starting their 30-year mortgage over again now in a more expensive home.

- Owning your home gives some tax advantages with mortgage interest payments being tax-deductible.

However, banks leverage mortgages more to their own favor than yours. Most loans are "Scheduled Interest," meaning the first 15 years of a mortgage the payments are 80 to 90% interest vs. principle. This means over 30 years you end up paying sometimes TRIPLE the value for your home.

Unless you can secure a really good DAILY AMORTIZED LOAN where you can make extra payments and have them actually apply toward the principle thereby reducing interest, it is hard to get ahead. For example: on a standard home loan with a $1000 monthly payment, $900 or more is going toward interest. In other words, your money is working for the bank rather than you. This leaves only $100 applied toward principal. The same $1000 monthly payment with a DAILY AMORTIZED LOAN can be split into bi-weekly (two per month) payments of $500. This can change the equation so upwards of $350 each month is going toward principal. Same monthly expense from your pocket book, but <u>cutting 7 to 10 years off your mortgage loan</u> and **saving you literally tens of thousands of dollars in interest!** The money saved can be applied toward your retirement. What is really powerful about a Daily amortized loan is if, the day after making your regular payment, you send in an extra payment, the extra payment is all applied to principal, reducing large amounts of interest. With a Scheduled interest loan, the payment is automatically applied to one of the last payments of the loan saving you very little interest. Dave Ramsey and Suze Orman talk about these things, but they don't tell you where to find the products.

Applying Rich Dad's Advice: Your Money Working for You!

This principle is simple on some accounts and quite complicated on others. For this reason, it is sound advice to have a good financial advisor. Find someone you can REALLY trust to coach you until you learn the basics for yourself. Time is working against you if you don't have the right counsel from the beginning.

There are numerous ways to make and invest money. Clearly, some work better than others and some do not work at all, thus costing you money.

Understanding the "Rule of 72," is a key principle for financial success. This should be taught in high school and tested frequently before graduating.

You simply take 72 and divide it by the interest rate you are receiving on your investment and it tells you how long it will take for your money to double.

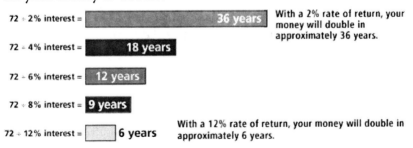

Graph Compliments of Primerica Financial Services

Remember, inflation is about 4.4%, so interest less than 4.4% means you are losing money!

Let's look at an example: If you put $100 in an investment at 2% and left it alone, in 36 years you would have $200. Taking inflation into consideration, it would be equivalent to $45.45 today. In actuality you would have lost half of the value of your money.

On the other hand, if you put that same $100 in a 12% yielding vehicle such as a Mutual Fund or ROTH IRA and left it alone for the same 36 years you would have $6400. WOW! Now that is having your money work for YOU!

With Loans (even your home loan) and credit card debts ranging from 6% to 19%, your money is working for someone other than you. Avoid debt whenever possible! Or learn how to be your own banker and make interest on loaning yourself money.

Combine and live by these three simple principles and you can build a debt-free, and financially independent, personal empire for yourself and your posterity.

The aforementioned is information I have learned through personal experience and financial advisors. Now days, several "financial gurus like Radio celebrity Dave Ramsey teach the same things. I wish I knew this stuff in my teens and twenties. Unfortunately, Dave and other celebrities can't tell you where to actually GET the products so ask around. Financial tools and products are always changing. A good tool this year might be less favorable or obsolete in a decade depending on new products or changes in the economic climate.

TECHNIQUES FOR ADVANCED LIVING
FINANCIAL SUMMARY:

"THE 5 PILLARS OF WEALTH" – Garrett Gunderson

- Balance your life between the 5 pillars of wealth:
  - Soul Purpose – Live your passion
  - Mental Capital – Invest in your knowledge
  - Social or Relationship Capital – Nurture your relationships
  - Health Capital – Be proactive not reactive about your health
  - Financial Capital – Build financial wealth but not at the expense of the other four pillars
- Live your wealth! Don't just save up for "someday" when you retire

"Owning a home is the first step toward building financial wealth."

- Purchase a home you can afford.
- Keep it clean and in good repair to increase it's value.
- Secure a good home loan that helps you pay off your home within 15 to 25 years without burden.
- Utilize the equity in your home to minimize debt and accelerate paying off your mortgage early.

Protect your family and your assets.

- Get quality affordable life insurance that will meet the surviving family member's needs without 'breaking the bank' while you are alive.
- TERM is the most affordable place to start.

- The right Whole-Life used to 'become your own bank" is a powerful wealth and confidence building tool. Counsel with a good agent.

Let your money work for you not someone else.

- Always pay yourself first! If you are a religious individual, tithing first and yourself second, but pay yourself or your retirement before you pay bills.

- Understand the Rule of 72. Paying yourself first over time is what builds your wealth.

- You are your best investment.

- Not all debt is bad, qualify your debts. A house can be a good debt. However...

- **Many argue that "Slavery" was abolished in the US. In my opinion, debt and long-term contractual agreements are nothing more than legalized slavery. When you are working to pay off high interest debts in your name, your time is not your own, your possessions purchased on credit are not really yours to keep and any money you make certainly is not 'working for you' but rather someone else.

- **You cannot build wealth while you are in debt. Pay off credit cards and other interest bearing debts early. If you use credit cards for sky miles, etc...make sure to pay-off the balance in full every month.

- Invest in books or coaches to help you in finance. The biggest mistake is guessing about your financial future.

  - Find Garrett Gunderson at wealthfactory.com

168

Footnotes:

58. U.S. Bureau of Census, Census 2000 Summary File=1.9. 2006=2.1, now suspected to be 2.3 but statistics lag by 2 years

59. *One-Child Policy* – China. See Wikipedia

PLANNED PARENTHOOD TO SOUTH KOREA: OOPS, WE DESTROYED YOU! SORRY! July 3, 2009

South Korea has the lowest birth rate and the fastest aging rate in the world. Population growth will reach 0% in 2019 but will continue to fall and turn into negative growth. The working age population will begin to fall in 2019. At the same time, the aging of workers will sharply increase. In the 1960's the Korean government, through Planned Parenthood of Korea, began to implement the one child per family policy, as 'economic development.'

We started in the sixties with a birth rate of 6.1 per couple. It is now 1.19. We should have stopped when the rate was 2.1 births per couple. We should have changed our policy. But we didn't…

60. In Europe 2.1 children per woman is considered to be the population replacement level. These are national averages

Ireland: 1.99

France: 1.90

Norway: 1.81

Sweden 1.75

UK: 1.74

Netherlands: 1.73

Germany: 1.37

Italy: 1.33

Spain: 1.32

Greece: 1.29

Source: Eurostat - 2004 figures

61. How Money Works, Secrets to Financial Success booklet - 2007 Primerica

EPILOGUE: SOLVING THE HEALTH AND WEALTH CONUNDRUM

Saving Money with Health Care Providers

One of the best decisions you can make in improving your health, wealth and the health of your family is to find a few good "Health Care Providers." Now I mean this in the strictest definition of the word. I am talking about Providers who treat the body as a whole, not chasing symptoms and pain. I am talking about Providers like Naturopathic doctors, Dentists, Nutritionists, Chiropractors, or the handful of Medical doctors who are educated in nutrition and herbs. I do not mean "Disease or Crisis Care Providers" who focus their practice on prescription drugs and surgery. Yes, these are important and necessary at times, however, if every time they see you they are prescribing another drug, then they are not helping you avoid Toxins. Prescriptions, in most cases, affect a symptom, not the cause. And prescriptions always have side-effects!

To quote Benjamin Franklin again, "An ounce of prevention is worth a pound of cure." This is true in four areas...mentally, physically, spiritually, and FINANCIALLY.

In Ancient China, the wealthier families had a personal family physician. The doctor made regular 'wellness checkups," to the home. *The physician was paid a fair exchange on a monthly basis as the family remained healthy.* Should someone in the family fall ill, the physician was called to attend to their needs. The physician would mix herbs, make diet and exercise recommendations or whatever he felt necessary to help restore the patient to health. The physician DID NOT, however, receive any payment for services WHILE a member of the family was sick. Rather, he was paid strictly in keeping his patients healthy. Now that is what I call, "Health Care."

Insurance

In today's world few people are willing to take responsibility for their own health. Everyone is looking for third party payment and transfer of responsibility in health / disease care. This type of thinking has, unfortunately, led our nation to a state of poor health, and our example is spreading rapidly to the free world. Simply put, our thinking is all wrong.

Common things doctors hear in America these days include:

"If my insurance doesn't cover it, I can't afford it."

> (And now we see insurance covers less and less while the cost of insurance is skyrocketing).

"I can't come to you; you are not on my insurance panel."

> (Should that matter if you have found a doctor you trust and they actually offer what you need for your health? If my car needs brakes and an oil change, but my warranty only covers the engine parts and transmission do I go somewhere else simply to have my transmission worked on since it is under my warranty? It makes no sense when we put

it in that perspective; yet people do this with their health every day in this country).

"My insurance said they would cover 80% after my co-pay. Why do I owe the hospital (or doctor) so much money?"

(Because insurance pays the percent based on *their own fee schedule,* not necessarily what the doctor or hospital charge for their services. Usually, with insurance, the patient is left with more owing than they expected).

Let me share a personal story regarding insurance…

HARRISON PART V FINANCE

When we took Harrison to the hospital to treat his Meningitis, it ended up being a financial fiasco. Being a physician, I had a few options to help us save money. One, I was allowed to administer the antibiotics to Harrison at home after one week in the hospital, rather than having him stay an entire month. Two, the pediatrician was a friend and lowered his fees. Other than that our options were no different than other families.

Harrison's medical expenses could have easily pushed $100K if he had stayed a month in the hospital. Luckily, I was able to keep it down to just $26,000. To my surprise, our family insurance was not willing to help with our new baby and his medical expenses. In other words; I, like many insured individuals, was left with the responsibility of ballooned medical bills and minimal or no insurance coverage. I may as well not have had any insurance at all.

After several days of frustration and arguing with our insurance carrier (to whom I paid a substantial chunk of my income each month), I finally called the hospital and said, "Forget insurance.

I want the cash price. What is it going to cost me to pay you myself without you having to use your billing department and chase your money with the insurance company?"

The lady at the hospital politely said, "Let me get back to you." When she returned my call the next day she had good news. "Mr. Shetlin," she said, "we are able to reduce the fees to just $5,000."

Wow! Insurance third party pay compounds expenses far over what is reasonable! Why? Because there are so many administrative fees, billing fees, postage, manpower, profits for share holders, and so much extra work and expense involved… the overhead is unbelievable.

For this reason, I strongly suggest finding "Health care providers" who cost-effectively keep you and your family healthy to reduce the personal expense of "disease care." Have insurance in place for **catastrophic** problems such as kidney failure, diabetes, loss of limb, cancer, etc. Naturally, we would use this kind of insurance as infrequently as possible…the way insurance is designed.

So, to save money and be protected, **have a high-deductible catastrophic insurance resulting in a lower monthly expense. Take the difference you are saving each month and put it in an investment earning 6% to 12% that is readily accessible.** This way your money is working for you! Then, if you need to meet your higher deductible for "disease care" or have need of a true "health care" expense, you simply deduct that from your 'invested' funds. If you remain healthy, then you are saving for your retirement or a 'rainy day' rather than paying/losing a sizeable amount of money each month for insurance that you rarely use and often doesn't cover what you need.

"Cash is king," whether buying a car, house or something at the flea market; paying with cash always gives you leverage for discounts. Health and Medical expenses are no different. Most Hospitals,

Urgent Care facilities, Orthodontists, Dentists, Chiropractors, Reconstructive Surgeons…you name it. . .offer large discounts for services rendered when a patient pays at the time of service or in advance and does not involve insurance / third party payers. Why? Because it saves so much work and expense all around, thus the provider can pass that savings to the patient.

Health clubs are a great example. You can go to a fancy gym for $20 per day. The average gym is about $10 per day. Or you can sign up for a year and it might be as little as $1 per day. **Commitment equals savings.** Buying health food supplies such as nutritional supplements, coconut oil, or anything really — when you purchase in bulk you save money. Do you see the pattern?

If insurance companies suddenly started paying for nutritional supplements or gym fees, on a fee-for-service basis like they do presently for our so called "health care," the price at the gym would skyrocket overnight, just like our pharmaceuticals and crisis/disease care has. Simply because the transfer of responsibility for payment now requires so much more time, work, and overhead for the provider or supplier to get paid.

Saving Money with Chiropractic

Statistics clearly show the healthiest people on the planet regularly see a Chiropractor.[62] Yes, Chiropractic is great for headaches and low back pain. Yes, it is fantastic for rehabilitation following a trauma such as an auto accident. However, if all you seek is a "Chiropractic aspirin" when you are in pain, you are missing the big picture…the *power of prevention.* Simply put, Chiropractic improves your quality of life, as well as, longevity. Not to mention, prevention and "true health care" can save your pocket book literally tens of thousands of dollars in "crisis or disease care."

Now, there are Chiropractors who focus on pain and there are Chiropractors who focus on wellness. Many balance their practice between the two.

When any joint in the body becomes stuck, blocked, or what we commonly term, "subluxated," the body responds with swelling or inflammation in that joint. The byproducts of inflammation are nerve irritating chemicals. The swelling of tissues involved can put unwanted pressure on nerves themselves or the inflammatory byproducts can irritate an adjacent nerve. A Chiropractic adjustment restores proper movement in a joint and helps to reduce inflammation and remove nerve interference.

It is necessary to point out that ONLY 10% OF THE NERVOUS SYSTEM has the job of SENSING PAIN. Therefore, when Chiropractors simply focus on the pain it is no different than chasing the symptom with medicine. 90% of the nervous system is busy coordinating millions of other body functions per second. The ninety-percentile nerves only send a pain signal if they are pinched 80% or more. Why? Because sending a pain signal is not their job.

For this reason, it is vitally important — for optimal health, healing, and well-being — that we keep our nervous system free of interference. It is even more important than brushing our teeth, getting 8 hours of sleep, or even a perfect diet. Now, I'm not saying don't brush your teeth, but if you get a cavity, it does not affect other organs and systems in your body.

If your organs are not getting 100% of the signal from the brain on how to function, how can they do their job efficiently?

Without 100% nerve function (blueprints), how well can the organs involved in the immune system prevent cancer and fight off a virus or bacterial infection? Did you know we each grow 10,000 cancer cells per day? It is the job of the complex immune system to recognize these irregular cells as 'non-self' and dispose of them properly. If our immune system is impeded even 10% by nerve interference, we are allowing 1000 cancer cells per day to flourish within our body. That is scary!

How about this:

- Statistically 1 in 4 people in the US die of cancer.
- 1 in 23 Chiropractic patients die of cancer.
- 1 in 300 chiropractors die of cancer.[63]

Really take a look at those numbers. How is this possible? I am a realist and I am not going to tell you that it is 100% Chiropractic adjustments that affect these numbers. It is a combination of things discussed in this book. But, as I said earlier in this section, people under regular Chiropractic care are some of the healthiest people on the planet. Why? Because CHIROPRACTIC is a lifestyle. It is not an event! It is not taking a pill for a symptom. Ah! Symptom is gone; I can ignore the other problems in my body because I no longer FEEL PAIN. The number of Chiropractic patients who die of cancer could be improved immensely, possibly to 1 in 100 if more patients pursued *wellness and prevention* instead of simply chasing away that ache or pain. Keeping your nervous system functioning at an optimal level, WHETHER OR NOT YOU FEEL PAIN, combined with proper nutrition, avoiding toxins and managing stress is the secret recipe everyone is looking for to obtain better health. Bonus, it is much more affordable than "crisis care."

Blueprints and Building Blocks

If we want to build a nice new building, it is vital we have a few quality basics in place.

First, we need a completed quality set of blueprints. Without the organization that blueprints provide it is difficult to keep on task from start to finish. It is difficult to have a group working toward the end goal at the same time. It is nearly impossible to orchestrate the project and certainly improbable to have a quality end product without quality "Blueprints."

Together with the blueprints we need quality building materials. For a commercial structure, that might include I-beams, mortar, windows, bricks, etc.

For our body, it is the correct molecular building blocks, in other words, our diet and nutrition. In either scenario, lack of quality in the building supplies results in a lack of quality for the end result, the structure. Since our body is under constant reconstruction we want to maximize the quality of the blueprints…Looking at the big picture, our brain houses the blueprints for the entire body, communicating with every living tissue through the spinal cord and nerves. On a cellular level it is the DNA. NOTE: We are building 300 Billion new cells per day and whether we have healthy DNA in those cells is also contingent on what we eat, in other words, the nutritional building blocks.

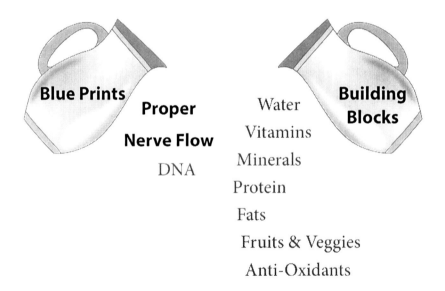

Blue Prints

Proper

Nerve Flow

DNA

Water

Vitamins

Minerals

Protein

Fats

Fruits & Veggies

Anti-Oxidants

Building Blocks

Picture a conveyor belt carrying a variety of organic building materials into a room titled "Cell Manufacturing." Since our body has a quota of 300 Billion new cells per day it has to produce no matter what. It will make new cells out of whatever materials are delivered on that conveyor belt. When we have poor habits of eating the same unhealthy processed foods daily, we continue to make less-than-perfect cells. Some of the things we eat in our "fast food" nation are simply unnatural.

I mentioned crispy, golden brown – French fries. They are almost an American staple. Unfortunately, in order to make them we have to cook potatoes (high starch) in oil (usually chemically altered by hydrogenation) at high temperatures. This creates molecules known as Trans-Fatty Acids. TFAs do not occur in nature, yet we ingest them and they end up on that conveyor belt going straight to "cell manufacturing." Because of the "daily quota" the body will use the TFA's to make new unhealthy cells. As a matter of fact, those cells can be carcinogenic or cause cancer.

It is vital that we get proper health promoting natural "building blocks" into our body on a regular basis…. Good building blocks "in" while keeping the toxins "out."

This is where individuals often become frustrated with the slow or minimally noticeable changes when they try a diet or exercise for a short period. For example:

"I started working out, but I didn't notice very much change."

"I tried working out, but it makes me feel sick; I don't have the energy."

"I tried eating better, but it cost too much money."

"It doesn't matter what I eat, my health or my weight doesn't change."

Of course it matters what we eat, the question is, will we as individuals make the RIGHT changes and continue on that course for a sustained period of time?

TECHNIQUE FOR ADVANCED LIVING

Save money with preventative thinking

- Learn and apply health and wealth practices. It is much more cost effective to "act" than to "react," to "prevent" vs. "chase a cure." Prevention is pro-active while "crisis management" is reactive and expensive.

Physicians

- Seek out physicians (Chiropractors or Medical Doctors) who have a 'Wellness' model of practice.

- Ask them if the have family wellness plans that are more effective and less expensive than using insurance.

- Get your family on a wellness model with these physicians (much like the Ancient China model), it will save you a fortune, and the entire family benefits

Footnotes:

62. Healthy people spend far less on life insurance, health insurance, even car insurance. Typically, the two largest expenses a family spends for are mortgage/rent and insurance.

63. I did not come up with these statistics but being licensed to practice chiropractic in Utah for 17+ years, I know there are just over 600 practicing chiropractors in the state and only 3 (in seventeen years) have died of cancer.

DEFINING "HEALTH" AND "WEALTH"

According to the World Health Organization, "Health is a state of complete physical, mental and social well-being and not merely the absence of disease or infirmity."

Wealth, on a purely financial plain could be defined as "the period of time a person can sustain their lifestyle if they stop working. An individual's wealth is therefore defined by three things: 1) their monthly expenses; 2) their liquid assets; and, 3) their passive income." By my definition and Garrett Gunderson's there are other aspects to wealth. He taught us the FIVE pillars of wealth. Financial wealth is only one pillar. Of course, what good is *financial wealth* without the *health* to enjoy it? In many ways, health and wealth are intertwined. Both require the passion and discipline to make the right choices again and again over time in order to maintaiwn or acquire further health and/or wealth.

Apply as many "Techniques for Advanced Living" to your daily life as possible and watch what happens. Implement one or two at a time. Master them then move on. You will be amazed at the increased peace, comfort, and abundance these habits will bring into your life. It may not happen overnight, but the recipe works. The more techniques you can properly master, the more health and wealth abundance will flow to you and through you mentally, spiritually, physically and financially.

Yours in Health and Wealth,

Dr. R. Jay Shetlin

RECOMMENDED READING & DVD'S

- "Natural Cures They Don't Want You to Know About," 2004, Kevin Trudeau
- "The Sanctity of Human Blood: Vaccine does not equal immunity." 2009 Tim O'Shea
- "What your doctor may NOT tell you about childhood vaccinations." 2001 Stephanie Cave, MD, Deborah Mitchell
- "Body for Life," Bill Phillips
- "Supersize me," DVD
- "Fast Food Nation," DVD
- "Total Health," Dr. Mercola
- "Discover Wellness," by Dr. Bob Hoffman
- "How to Raise a Healthy Child in Spite of Your Doctor," 1984 Robert Mendelsohn, MD
- "The Metabolic Plan," Stephen Cherniske, MS
- "The biology of Belief," Bruce H Lipton, PhD
- "How Money works," Secrets to Financial Success
- "Killing Sacred Cows," Garrett Gunderson
- Other "Conundrum" Books — www.drjayshetlin.com

RECOMMENDED SOURCES

Six o'clock scramble

On-line fast and healthy meals — http://thescramble.com/

Healthy Recipes

Articles — www.shetlin.com

Top 10 Goals (Write them down, make them real)

1._____

_____

2._____

_____

3._____

_____

4._____

_____

5._____

_____

6._____

_____

7._____

_____

8._____

_____

9._____

_____

10._____

_____

Add some more goals (get crazy…'spend the night in a space station', 'swim the English channel'…)

_____

_____

_____

_____

_____

_____

_____

_____

_____

_____

_____

_____

_____

_____

Write 3 sub-goals for each of your 10 key goals...sub-goals are the little steps you need to take in order to make the big goals really happen.

1._____

2._____

3._____

1._____

2._____

3._____

1._____

2._____

3._____

1._____

2._____

3._____

1._____

2._____

3._____

FUTURE HEALTH

1._____

2._____

3._____

1._____

2._____

3._____

1._____

2._____

3._____

1._____

2._____

3._____

1._____

2._____

3._____

1._____

2._____

3._____

List all the traumas you have had in your life. Big traumas like broken bones, surgeries, or car accidents. Little traumas like repetitive micro-traumas of poor posture, sitting at a computer all day, etc.

_____

_____

_____

_____

_____

_____

_____

_____

_____

_____

_____

_____

_____

Have you ever had them checked by a professional? Are you doing anything to prevent scar tissue build-up or unhealthy posture
changes that could rob you of quality of life and longevity?

_____

_____

_____

_____

_____

_____

What action steps are you going to take to improve your intake
"building blocks?"

_____

_____

_____

_____

_____

_____

_____

What action steps are you going to take to minimize your intake of "toxins?"

_____

_____

_____

_____

_____

_____

What action steps are you going to take to increase regular exercise in your life?

_____

_____

_____

_____

_____

_____

NOTES:

NOTES:

_____

_____

_____

_____

_____

_____

_____

_____

_____

_____

_____

_____

_____

_____

_____

_____

OTHER BOOKS BY DR. JAY SHETLIN

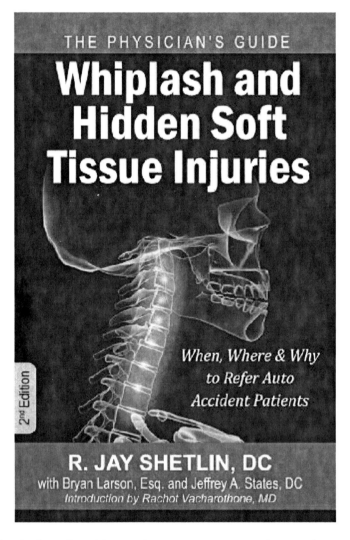

Whiplash and Hidden Soft Tissue Injuries: When, Where and Why to refer Auto Accident Patients

Solving the Health and Wealth Conundrum

The Science and Religion of Nutrition

CPSIA information can be obtained
at www.ICGtesting.com
Printed in the USA
FFOW02n0410080218
44891668-45082FF

9 780984 390045